A STEP-BY-STEP GUIDE TO
Houseplant Care

This edition published 1992 by
  Whitecap Books Ltd.
  1086 West 3rd Street
  North Vancouver, B.C.
  Canada V7P 3J6
© 1992 Colour Library Books Ltd.,
Godalming, Surrey, England
Printed and bound in Singapore by Tien Wah Press
ISBN 1 55110 043 6

A STEP-BY-STEP GUIDE TO
Houseplant Care

Text by
DAVID SQUIRE

Photography by
NEIL SUTHERLAND

WHITECAP BOOKS

CONTENTS

Section I – Houseplant Care

Introduction 10

Selecting and Buying 12

Pots and Compost 14

Light and Warmth 16

Need for Water 18

Humidity 22

Repotting 24

Feeding and Top-Dressing 26

Grooming and Care 28

Propagation 30

Physiological Disorders 90

Potting Bulbs and Corms 60

Planting a Bottle Garden 66

Creating Terraria 68

Indoor Hanging Baskets 70

Hydroculture 72

Bonsai 74

Indoor Herbs 80

Holiday Care 82

Houseplant Pests 86

Houseplant Diseases 88

Section II – Houseplant Guide

Introduction 92

Flowering Trailers and Cascaders 94

Flowering Climbers 96

Climbing Foliage Plants 98

Trailing and Cascading Foliage Plants 100

Architectual Plants 102

Scented Houseplants 104

Acknowledgements 124

Insectivorous Plants 106

Houseplants with Berries and Fruits 108

Plants for Bright Places 110

Plants for Soft Light 112

Plants for Shaded Areas 114

Glossary of Terms 118

Index 120

Houseplant Care

Selecting and buying, watering and feeding, potting, propagating and displaying houseplants are fundamental facets of growing plants indoors, as well as in greenhouses, conservatories and sunrooms.

Growing plants in small pots in rooms, greenhouses or conservatories is not easy. Outdoors – and when planted in the ground – the yearly cycle of seasons strongly influences growth and plants are always in harmony with their surroundings. Indoors, however, plants are expected to thrive and create eye-catching displays although often living in conditions alien to them. Frequently there is a wide range of plants in a room, all demanding different temperatures and amounts of light. And although plants can be selected to suit varying amounts of light in a room, they all usually have to survive in the same temperature, which may radically vary during winter when heating is turned off at night.

The first part of this all-colour book reveals the skills needed to look after houseplants, including what to look for when buying them, ways to judge if water is needed, feeding, top-dressing and repotting.

Houseplant enthusiasts invariably want to increase their plants but often believe it is difficult. Here, the techniques of propagating these plants is revealed in step-by-step pictures that enable everyone confidently to sow seeds, divide congested plants and to take cuttings, whether formed of leaves, stems and leaves, or fat and perhaps woody stems.

Displaying houseplants in eye-catching and unusual ways is as equally important as growing them successfully. These range from displaying plants singly or in groups to planting them in indoor hanging-baskets, bottles and terrariums.

Bonsai plants were originally miniature trees, shrubs and conifers kept dwarf in shallow containers. And although they could be taken indoors for a couple of days at one time they were basically outdoor plants. Today, however, there is an increasing range of bonsai that can be grown indoors throughout the year. The art of growing both types of bonsai is explained and illustrated.

Choosing and buying plants for the home, greenhouse and conservatory requires as much care as when buying any other item. Buying a low-cost plant that dies during the following week makes it an expensive buy.

DON'T BUY PLANTS...

- with roots coming out of the drainage hole.
- with wilting leaves. It indicates too dry or too wet potting compost.
- without labels.
- that are displayed in cold and draughty positions, as their buds may later drop off.
- that are infested with pests and diseases.
- with compost covered in green slime.
- with bare stems and few leaves.
- growing in small pots but having large amounts of foliage. Conversely, don't buy small plants in large pots.

Above: *Plants with roots coming out of drainage holes in their pots indicates that repotting is needed. If left for too* long in this starved condition, plants seldom recover and will not be attractive.

Above: *Moss on pots indicates that the plant has remained too long in its pot and that growth may have been restricted. Although the moss can be removed, the plant may not recover.*

Above: *Small plants in large pots are difficult to water. When roots do not fill most of the pot, potting compost often* becomes stagnant. Conversely, large plants in small pots are deprived of essential nutrients for growth.

Above: *Plants bought while in full bloom – or with faded flowers – only remain attractive for a limited period.* Only buy flowering plants that have plenty of flower buds still to open. Inspect the plant carefully.

TAKING PLANTS HOME

Houseplants – as well as those for greenhouses and conservatories – can only be a success if they arrive home safely and quickly become established in their new environment.

• Get your plants home and unwrapped as quickly as possible.
• Place newly-bought plants in moderate warmth, out of direct and strong sunlight.
• Don't knock flowering plants, as their buds may then fall off.
• Ensure that the compost is moist – but not waterlogged.
• About a week after being taken home, move the plant to its permanent position. Do not keep moving it, especially if delicate.
• If a few leaves or buds initially fall off, do not worry, as the plant is probably just settling down.

Above: *Plants that are in a poor state of health never recover, irrespective of how much care and attention they are subsequently given. Stems that have lost their leaves never again become properly clothed.*

Above: *Healthy houseplants enrich a home for many months, sometimes years. Damaged plants, as well as those infested with pests and diseases, inevitably engender disappointment. The first step to success with houseplants is to inspect them carefully before buying, and then to get them home safely and quickly.*

Pots and potting compost are essential to growing plants indoors. Traditional pots for plants were made of clay, but during recent decades plastic ones have gained supremacy. However, both types enable plants to grow healthily, and both have advantages and disadvantages.

CLAY POTS ...

- usually break when dropped.
- are much heavier that plastic types and therefore create a firm base for large plants.
- are more difficult to clean than plastic types.
- that are dry must be soaked in water before use.
- are a natural colour and harmonize with all plants.
- have a porous nature that allows damaging salts to escape from the potting compost – especially important if plants are fed excessively.
- encourage potting compost to remain cool in summer and warm in winter.
- are usually used in conjunction with loam-based potting composts.

PLASTIC POTS ...

- are light and easy to handle.
- become brittle with age, especially if stored outdoors and at low temperatures.
- are not porous and therefore the potting compost needs less frequent watering.
- do not need to have broken pieces of pots put in their bases, unlike clay types.
- are usually used in conjunction with peat-based potting composts.
- are available in a wide colour range and are well suited to harmonizing with modern design settings.

Range of sizes
Both clay and plastic pots are sold in a range of sizes, from 5cm/2in to about 38cm/15in wide. These measurements

Above: *Both clay and plastic pots – as well as loam-based and peat-based potting composts – grow healthy plants. Loam types are usually in clay pots (left) and peat types in plastic pots (right).*

indicate the distance across the inside at the pot's top. The depth of a pot is about the same as the width. Small pots increase in 12mm/½in stages, larger ones in 2.5cm/1in or 5cm/2in increments.

Cache pots
Also known as cover pots, they surround growing pots, creating an attractive feature as well as complementing and high-lighting home decor. Most are round, plain or decorated, and in a wide colour range. However, some – and especially larger types – are square, with the largest mounted on castors.

Additional to those sold specially as cache pots, many old home artefacts – perhaps from granny's attic – create interesting features.

The prime danger with cache pots is

Right: *The pot should be in balance with the size of the plant, as shown here. Avoid large plants in small pots, and small plants in large pots, as it makes watering them very difficult.*

that when plants are watered, excess water may remain in their bases and eventually cause roots to decay. Therefore, about ten minutes after watering a plant, tip away water in the cache pot's base.

Saucers
Because growing pots have holes in their bases to allow excess water to drain, they must be stood in saucers – or placed in cache pots – to prevent water spoiling decorative surfaces.

They are available in a wide range of colours and designs, some matching the growing pot to create a co-ordinated design.

Potting composts (potting soils)
Garden soil is not suitable for growing plants in pots indoors, as it is variable in quality, often badly drained and may contain weed seeds, pests and diseases.

Specially-prepared potting composts are needed and basically there are two types – 'loam-based' and 'peat-based'. However, plants can be grown without any potting compost and this is known as hydroculture, also known as hydroponics (see pages 72 and 73).

Loam-based potting composts are formed from sterilized soil, sharp sand and peat, whereas peat-based types are wholly created from peat. Both have advantages and disadvantages.

LOAM-BASED TYPES ...

- are heavier than peat-types and therefore give greater stability to large plants.
- are unlikely to dry out so fast or so completely as peat-based types.
- have a larger reserve of minor and trace plant foods than peat-based potting composts.
- will grow most houseplants, but the loam must have been properly sterilized.

PEAT-BASED TYPES ...

- are more uniform than clay-based types (the quality of the loam is frequently variable).
- are relatively light to carry home and are easily stored by sealing the bag and keeping it in a dry, cool place.
- are suitable for most plants, but feeding is needed at an earlier stage than with loam-based types.
- dry out quicker than soil-based potting composts, and are more difficult to remoisten if watering has been neglected.

Above: *Garden soil* **Below:** *Peat-based compost*

Above: *Houseplants in garden soil (left) under achieve. Both loam-based (centre) and peat-based potting composts (right) successfully grow healthy houseplants.*

Right: *Loam-based compost*

Light and warmth – in Nature provided by sunlight – are vital for healthy growth, activating the growing process in plants. In Nature, light and warmth are in harmony and balance, the temperature rising with an increase in light intensity.

There is also a close relationship between the seasons and light and warmth. Plants indoors, however, are often expected to thrive in high temperatures and low light.

REMEMBER ...

• Plants vary enormously in their need for light. On pages 110 to 115 a range of plants is suggested for three different light intensities – bright places, soft light, and shaded areas.
• The intensity of light varies from season to season, and plants that can be positioned on a south-facing windowsill in winter may need a north-facing window in summer.
• The intensity of light decreases rapidly as the distance from a window increases. For example, at 2.4m/8ft from a window the light is 5-10% of that on a windowsill.
• Full sun – especially in summer –

scorches the leaves of most houseplants except cacti and other succulents.
• Flowering plants need more light than those just grown for their foliage.
• Plants placed close to windows in winter, to enable them to gain maximum light, may suffer from cold draughts if windows are ill-fitting, causing flower buds to drop off.
• Plants should not be suddenly moved from a dull position into very strong light. Instead, gradually accustom them to better light.
• Keep windows clean when light intensity is low. In summer, net curtains help to diffuse strong light.

Artificial lighting

Houseplant enthusiasts who live in basements or dark-roomed houses can use 'growing lights' suspended over plants to supplement low light. This is especially useful in winter to keep plants healthy and growing. The light source is suspended 15-30cm/6-12in above flowering plants, and 30-60cm/1-2ft above those primarily grown for their attractive foliage.

Use the lights about twelve hours each day. Do not leave them on all night.

Above: *Strong light is just as harmful as too little. This peperomia has been exposed to strong light, causing leaves to wilt and shrivel. Thick-leaved plants are less affected than thin-leaved types.*

*The peperomia **above** has been given slight shade, especially in summer.*

Above: *Plants that are deprived of light become unsightly and eventually deteriorate to a point where recovery is impossible. This variegated plant has been kept in a dark position,*

*unlike the plant **above** that has been grown in good light.*

Above: *Leaves form blisters when water droplets fall on them and they are then exposed to strong sunlight. The water acts as a lens, intensifying the light and burning the leaf.*

Above: *Plants naturally grow towards light, their stems and leaves bending over in an unsightly manner. Therefore, every few days turn foliage plants a quarter of a turn. Plants that are*

Above: *Rapidly changing temperatures between day and night – and especially within the period of light – soon cause leaves to fall off. Too wet or dry compost also contributes to the fall of leaves. Plants with thicker and tougher*

*leaves, such as the ivy **above**, are not damaged so severely.*

Above: *High temperatures, low humidity and dry potting compost cause plants to wilt and the foliage to shrivel. Leaves become crisp and dry, eventually falling off and creating an unsightly plant. However, plants that are placed in*

*more conducive conditions retain their glossy leaves as **above**.*

Above: *Growing a plant in low temperatures is just as damaging as in those that are too high. The plant ceases to grow, eventually collapsing – leaves and flowers around the outside are affected first. Getting the temperature right makes a difference in a plant's growth, as indicated **right**.*

*turned regularly have an even outline, as **above**.*

Like all living things, plants are formed mainly of water, and without it they soon die. Plants absorb water through small, hair-like roots. The moisture moves into larger roots and then to stems and eventually leaves. From there it passes through small pores known as stoma – mainly found on the undersides of the leaves – into the atmosphere. This is known as transpiration, and as well as keeping the plant cool, firm and upright, it enables the absorption of plant foods from the potting compost and its subsequent movement within a plant.

JUDGING IF A PLANT NEEDS WATER
More houseplants die through being excessively or insufficiently watered than from any other reason. Judging when a plant in a pot needs water is a skill derived from experience, although in recent years specialized equipment has taken the guesswork out of this task.

3 Tapping a clay pot with a cotton-reel (bobbin) attached to a short stick indicates the degree of moisture: the pot rings if water is needed, but is dull when wet. Only works on clay pots.

4 Moisture-indicator strips – also known as watering signals – are relatively new. They are inserted into potting compost and the need for moisture is indicated by the strip.

1 Rubbing a finger or thumb on potting compost to assess its moisture content is the most popular method of judging if water is needed. However, repeated pressing tends to compress the compost.

2 The colour of potting compost indicates if water is needed. When dry, it becomes pale and crumbly, but if wet is dark. Eventually, most houseplant enthusiasts use this method to assess if water is needed.

APPLYING WATER TO HOUSEPLANTS

Plants are individual in their need for water, some requiring more than others. Large plants need more water than small ones, while in winter and when dormant they need less water than in summer. Also, large plants in small pots need more frequent watering than small plants in large pots. There are two main ways in which to water houseplants.

1 Watering 'over the rim' is the usual way to apply water, filling the space between the potting compost and rim. Allow excess to filter through to a saucer, emptying it after half an hour.

2 Soft and hairy leaves are damaged if water falls on them. Water by standing the pot in a bowl of water until moisture reaches the surface. Then remove and allow excess to drain.

5 Moisture-meters are widely available and indicate when soil or compost needs water. They are very efficient and precise, but repeated insertions of the probe eventually damages the plant's roots.

Too much or too little water

When garden plants are watered, excess soon percolates downwards, and unless the area is waterlogged the roots do not become drowned and deprived of air. Potting compost, however, soon becomes dry in summer, while in winter, when a plant is not growing rapidly, it may become waterlogged if too much water is applied to the compost.

Both dry and water-saturated potting compost causes plants to wilt. An inspection soon reveals the cause.

Leaves are the food-producing parts of plants. They use carbon-dioxide from the atmosphere, in combination with water absorbed by the roots, to create growth. This process is activated by sunlight and is known as photosynthesis. Water also passes into the atmosphere through small holes (singly known as stoma, collectively as stomata). In most plants these are mainly found on the undersides of leaves. Water given off in this way is known as transpiration.

Water, together with plant foods, passes into the large roots, then to stems and later into leaves. Some plants have long stems, while others have leaves that appear to develop from a point level with the surface of the potting compost or soil.

Roots are vital to plants. Large roots hold a plant firmly in the soil or potting compost, while fine ones absorb water, as well as the nutrients mixed in it. The water then passes through the larger roots on its way to the stems and leaves.

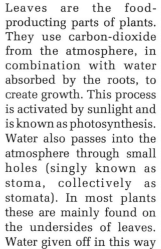

SAVING A DRY PLANT

1 Plants deprived of water will wilt, eventually reaching a point when, no matter how much water is given, they never recover. Leaves and stems first become soft, then dry and crisp.

SAVING AN OVER WATERED PLANT

1 If the compost is saturated, leaves become limp and eventually slime covers the potting compost and diseases infest the plant. Lower leaves are the first to become diseased and unsightly.

2 *Plants can be revived if action is taken rapidly. If it has flowers, cut them off. Foliage plants can be* immediately stood in a bowl of water until bubbles cease to rise from the dry compost.

3 *Mist-spray the leaves several times to reduce the plant's need to absorb water to replenish that lost by* moisture escaping to the atmosphere through its leaves. Place in light shade for a few days.

2 *Knock the pot's rim on a firm surface and remove the pot. If the soil-ball is packed with roots it will retain its shape, but if sparse there is the risk of it falling apart. Take care not to damage the roots.*

3 *Use absorbent kitchen towel to soak up excess water from the soil-ball. Several repeated wrappings may be necessary to remove the water – and check if root mealy bugs (like small woodlice) are present.*

4 *Leave the soil-ball wrapped in absorbent paper until dry – but not bone-dry and crumbly. If the soil-ball is packed with roots, it is better to leave it unwrapped and exposed to the air to allow excess moisture to evaporate.*

5 *When the soil-ball is dry, pot up the plant into fresh potting compost and a clean pot. Resume normal watering, but take care not continually to saturate the compost, as the plant may be seriously damaged.*

Humidity

The amount of moisture in the air influences the health and growth of plants. Desert cacti live in arid and hot regions and have thick outer layers that reduce the amount of moisture they give off. Most plants, however, need a humid atmosphere if their leaves and stems are not to become dry.

The perceived humidity of air is closely related to the temperature. The higher the temperature, the larger the amount of moisture it can hold. In winter, when the air is quite dry, rooms in which the temperature is high can, as far as plants are concerned, become like deserts. This is not a problem for cacti, but jungle plants soon suffer — both flowering and foliage types.

EXCESSIVE HUMIDITY

- Soft leaves soon decay, especially if hairy. Moisture becomes trapped around the hairs.
- Leaves that clasp stems create traps for water.
- Flower petals, especially when tightly packed together, become covered with a furry mould.
- Plants with masses of soft leaves closely packed together become infested with decay.

DRY ATMOSPHERE

- Tips of leaves become shrivelled, curled and brown.
- The whole plant wilts if the temperature is very high, with leaves eventually falling off.
- Flowers fade and discolour, with flower buds wilting and eventually falling off.
- Surfaces of leaves become dull.
- Tips of shoots wilt, then shrivel.

1 Placing plants in groups creates humid micro-climates around them. Moisture given off from the surfaces of leaves is trapped. When a plant is displayed on its own, moisture soon disperses.

2 Regularly mist-spray smooth-surfaced leaves in summer. However, take care not to spray water on flowers, as they then soon decay. Place a piece of card in front of flowers.

3 A few plants – such as philodendrons and the Swiss Cheese Plant – have aerial roots that must be mist-sprayed in summer to prevent them becoming dry and hard.

DON'T MIST-SPRAY ...

- when the sun is shining. Water globules act as lenses, intensifying the sun's rays and burning leaves.
- during evenings, especially in autumn and winter. Instead, mist-spray in the morning, so that moisture has a chance to dry before the onset of night.

DOUBLE-POTTING

Some foliage houseplants can be given both a humid atmosphere and cool roots by potting them in two pots, one inside the other. A layer of moist peat between the pots protects the potting compost from excessive warmth, while the moist peat creates humidity around the leaves.

Only clay pots can be used for double-potting, as the cooling is created by the evaporation of moisture through the sides of pots. Plastic pots do not allow this to happen.

1 Select a clay pot about 5cm/2in wider than the clay pot in which a plant is growing. Place moist peat in its base and put the smaller one inside. The two rims must be level.

2 Fill the space between them with moist peat. It is usually necessary to use a small stick to compress the peat. Ensure that the inner pot is in the centre of the outer one.

3 Use a small jug to moisten the peat between the pots. Allow excess water to drain, ensuring the peat is not totally saturated. Regularly check that the peat is moist, especially in summer.

Repotting

When plants fill their pots with roots they must be repotted. To neglect this task results in a plant becoming stunted and not achieving its full size.

It is essential that plants are progressively moved only in small stages from one pot to a larger one. If small plants are moved into too large pots, their roots are then surrounded by masses of potting compost and it is difficult to keep the moisture content at the right level. When potting compost in a pot is filled with roots, excess moisture is rapidly absorbed and given off by the plant through the leaves, preventing the potting compost becoming completely saturated and eventually making it totally unsuitable for plants.

REPOTTING CACTI

Many cacti have stiff and sharp spines and therefore need to be handled carefully. When repotting them either use gloves or hold the plant firmly by encircling it with a band formed of folded newspapers (below).

1 Thoroughly water the plant a few days before repotting it – a dry soil-ball does not encourage rapid establishment. Tap the pot's rim on a firm surface while supporting the soil-ball.

3 Place some potting compost in the pot's base, so that the surface of the root-ball is about 12mm/½in below the new pot's rim. Then, trickle potting compost over and around the plant's root-ball.

2 Check that the roots are healthy and not infested by root pests, such as root mealy bugs (see pages 84 to 87). Select a clean pot that is slightly larger than the previous one.

4 Gently firm potting compost around the root-ball until it is 12mm/½in below the rim. Later in the plant's life, when larger pots are used, leave a larger space at the top.

5 Water the potting compost 'over the rim', rather than by standing the pot in a bowl shallowly filled with water. Watering overhead in this way settles compost around the roots. It is essential they are in close contact. To improve the plant's appearance, place the growing pot in an attractive outer container, known as a cache pot.

Plants need a balanced diet of nutrients if they are to remain healthy and live for a long time. Most plants under-achieve, as they are usually starved. Regular feeding during a plant's growing period can make a remarkable difference. Both foliage and summer-flowering houseplants are normally fed from early spring to late summer (at 10-14 day intervals), while they are growing strongly. Winter-flowering plants, however, can be fed at about 14-day intervals during the period they remain in flower.

Plants need different amounts of foods at certain times in their development; to create a strong root-system (phosphates), masses of leaves and stems (nitrogen), or a wealth of flowers (potash).

Houseplants are usually bought when young and perhaps still using the nutrients in the potting compost into which they were initially potted. Once they have completely used this food supply they need regular feeding.

WAYS TO FEED PLANTS IN POTS

Liquid fertilizers
This is the traditional and most common way to feed house-plants. Concentrated fertilizers are diluted in clean water and applied to the potting compost at ten to

1 Before using a liquid fertilizer, carefully read the instructions. Never use more fertilizer than that recommended by the manufacturer.

2 Thoroughly agitate the water, ensuring that the fertilizer is completely mixed. Use before the plant food has had time to settle.

3 Do not apply liquid fertilizers to dry compost as it may then damage roots or run out of the gap between the soil-ball and inside the pot.

fourteen-day intervals during summer. Do not experiment with the concentration – it may kill your plants.

If the potting compost is dry, first water it. This is because when it is dry there is a risk of the fertilizer damaging the roots. Also, if it is dry the soil-ball contracts and leaves a gap around the inside of the pot, through which water and fertilizer will escape and be wasted.

Fertilizer pills and sticks
These are pushed into the potting compost and provide food over several months. They are best used in spring and up to midsummer. Once applied, they continue to give off plant foods until expired; if applied late in summer and into autumn they provide food when some plants are supposed to be resting.

Unlike liquid fertilizers, which spread fertilizer over all the potting compost, pills and sticks concentrate the nutrients in one position and encourage an uneven spread of roots. However, they are easy and clean to use.

Foliar feeding plants
As well as absorbing nutrients through their roots, some plants are able to take in foods through their leaves. Plants usually respond quickly to foliage feeds and therefore the technique is best used as a quick, pick-me-up tonic.

Liquid plant food is diluted with clean water and applied through a mist-sprayer. Only foliar feed plants with smooth, non-hairy leaves – and avoid spraying flowers. Also, do not mist-spray plants when they are in strong sunlight.

4 Lightly misting the leaves of some plants with a weak mixture of water and liquid fertilizer is possible where the leaves are smooth – not hairy.

5 Gently push a feeding stick into the compost, about 12mm/½in in from the pot's side, as this is where most of the feeding roots are situated.

6 Pills can also be inserted into the compost. Some devices enable pills to be inserted without having to dirty your hands on the compost.

TOP-DRESSING LARGE HOUSEPLANTS

1 *When plants in pots become too large to be repotted, they are topdressed in spring. Allow the surface* *soil to dry slightly, then use a small trowel to scrape away the top 2.5-3.6cm/1-1½in*

2 *Replace the surface scrapings with fresh potting compost. Leave a space between the top of the compost* *and the rim, so that the plant can be watered when the potting compost becomes dry.*

FEEDING AIR PLANTS AND BROMELIADS

1 *Air-plants (Tillandsias) are adapted to live in humid places. Feed by misting the leaves with a weak solution (about a quarter of the normal strength solution) of a liquid fertilizer once a month from spring to late summer.*

2 *Many bromeliads have urns at their centres, through which they are watered and fed. Once a month from spring to late summer, pour a weak solution (about a quarter of the normal strength) of a liquid fertilizer into the urn.*

BENEFITS OF FEEDING

1 *Regularly feeding houseplants makes a remarkable difference. Here are two Mexican Hat (Bryophyllum daigremontianum) plants, propagated at the same time. The one on the left has* *not been fed, other than the nutrients it gained when initially potted; the one on the right has been fed regularly, every 14 days.*

27

Grooming plants so they look their best is an essential part of growing houseplants. By the removal of dead flowers the flowering period can be extended. Also, the removal of shoot tips encourages a neat and attractive plant, while supporting and training stems also creates a neat appearance.

TRAINING A PINK JASMINE

1 From early autumn to late spring, the Pink Jasmine (Jasminum polyanthum) creates a wealth of white or pale-pink flowers, usually trained around a large hoop of pliable canes, or a white or green plastic loop.

2 When young plants have shoots 25-45cm/10-18in long, insert the support into the potting compost. Pliable canes are just pushed into it, while plastic loops are attached to the rim.

3 Carefully curl and train shoots around the support, taking care not to bend or kink them. Repeat this task several times throughout summer, and regularly feed the plant to encourage growth.

CLEANING LEAVES

Dust and dirt are the enemies of leaves, spoiling their appearance, clogging pores and preventing the sun reaching them. Proprietary, ozone-friendly sprays are available, and these are ideal for large-leaved plants, while hairy-leaved types and bristly cacti can be cleaned with a small soft brush.

1 Support large leaves with one hand and gently wipe with a damp cloth or spray with a leaf-cleaner. Do not do this when the plant is in strong sunlight.

2 Clean plants with many small leaves by gently swirling them in a bowl of clean water, allowing excess to drain, and dry in gentle warmth but away from direct and strong sunlight.

3 Remove dirt and dust from bristly cacti, as well as hairy-leaved plants, by using a small, soft brush. Blowing strongly on leaves while brushing also helps to remove dirt.

LOOKING AFTER FLOWERS

Flowering houseplants, as well as those in greenhouses and conservatories, need regular checking when bearing flowers. Decaying flowers left on plants encourage others to rot, and the decay may then spread to soft leaves. Also, the removal of dead flowers encourages the development of others.

1 Pinch off dead flowers from azaleas. Do not leave parts of flowers, as this encourages the onset of decay around soft shoots. Hold the shoot firmly while carrying out this task.

2 Pull off the stems of cyclamen flowers that have faded and started to wither. Hold the stem firmly and tug sharply, so that it comes away from the plant's base. Do not just remove the flowers.

TRIMMING STEMS AND SHOOTS

Some plants have a sprawling, scrambling and climbing nature and although this is often part of their attraction occasionally stems need to be trimmed. Always trim them back to a leaf-joint, using a sharp knife, secateurs, scissors or just by holding the stem firmly and snapping it sideways. Never leave a short piece of stem, as this encourages the onset of decay.

1 Slightly woody stems, such as those on azaleas, are best trimmed with sharp scissors, cutting back to a leaf-joint. This encourages bushiness and the development of sideshoots.

2 Encourage young plants to form a bushy base by nipping back young shoots to leaf-joints. If this job is neglected, plants become bare at their bases and unappealing.

Many houseplants can be increased from seeds, whether grown for their flowers, foliage or berries. Others include palms, ferns, insectiverous plants, cacti and other succulents. Whatever the type of plant, the seeds need three basic conditions to encourage germination — moisture, warmth and air. Most seeds germinate in darkness, but a few — such as the Wax Flower (*Begonia semperflorens*) — need light.

These conditions are created by sowing seeds in a seed compost that both retains moisture yet allows air penetration, and either placing in a greenhouse or on a warm windowsill indoors. Propagation cases with warmth provided by electric cables ensure an even and uniform temperature. Seed packets usually indicate the correct temperature, but in general one about 16-21°C/61-70°F is suitable.

There are many houseplants that can be increased in this way and some popular ones are suggested here.

Houseplants to increase from seeds
Flowering houseplants
- *Achimenes*
Hot Water Plant

Calceolaria hybrida – Slipper Flower

- *Begonia semperflorens*
Wax Flower
- *Calceolaria hybrida*
Slipper Flower/Pocketbook Plant
- *Cyclamen persicum*
Cyclamen
- *Exacum affine*
Persian Violet
- *Impatiens walleriana*
Busy Lizzie
- *Kalanchoe blossfeldiana*
Flaming Katy
- *Primula malacoides*
Poison Primula/Fairy Primrose
- *Saintpaulia ionantha*
African Violet
- *Schizanthus pinnatus*
Butterfly Flower
- *Senecio cruentus*
Cineraria
- *Strelitzia reginae*
Bird of Paradise Flower

Foliage houseplants
- *Begonia rex*
Rex Begonia
- *Cissus antarctica*
Kangaroo Vine
- *Coleus blumei*
Flame Nettle/Coleus

- *Cordyline australis*
Cabbage Palm
- *Cyperus alternifolius*
Umbrella Plant
- *Dizygotheca elegantissima*
False Aralia
- *Ficus benjamina*
Weeping Fig

Howeia forsteriana – Kentia Palm

- *Grevillea robusta*
Silky Oak
- *Hypoestes phyllostachya*
Polka Dot Plant
- *Mimosa pudica*
Sensitive Plant
- *Monstera deliciosa*
Swiss Cheese Plant
- *Ricinus communis*
Castor Oil Plant

Palms for the home
- *Chamaedorea elegans*
Parlour Palm
- *Chamaedorea seifrizii*
Reed Palm
- *Chamaerops humilis*
European Fan Palm
- *Chrysalidocarpus lutescens*
Areca Palm
- *Howeia forsteriana*
Kentia Palm
- *Washingtonia filifera*
Washington Fan Palm

Ferns for the home
- *Asparagus densiflorus* 'Meyeri'
Plume Asparagus
- *Asparagus densiflorus* 'Sprengeri'
Asparagus Fern
- *Asparagus setaceus*
Asparagus Fern
- *Asplenium nidus*
Bird's Nest Fern
- *Pellaea rotundifolia*
Button Fern
- *Platycerium bifurcatum*
Stag's Horn Fern

Fruiting houseplants
- *Ardisia crenata*
Coral Berry
- *Capsicum annuum*
Christmas Pepper
- *Solanum capsicastrum*
Winter Cherry

Insectiverous plants
- *Darlingtonia californica*
Hooded Pitcher Plant
- *Drosera capensis*
Sundew Plant
- *Drosera rotundifolia*
Sundew Plant
- *Sarracenia purpurea*
Pitcher Plant

Cacti and succulents
Collections of seeds are available, as well as specific species.

HELPING SEEDS TO GERMINATE

Some seeds are difficult to germinate, but there are ways to overcome this problem:
- Hard seed-coats prevent rapid germination.
- Either shallowly nick the hard coat with a sharp knife, or rub with sandpaper.
- Most seeds germinate in a constant temperature, but some respond to fluctuations in the warmth.
- Cold periods encourage some seeds to germinate. It makes them believe winter has passed and spring has arrived, a natural time for germination.

SOWING SEEDS

1 Fill a clean plastic seed-tray with seed compost. If small numbers of seeds are to be sown, use a shallow seed pan. Do not sow different seeds in the same containers.

2 Using your fingers, firm the seed compost, especially around the sides and edges as this is where it will start to become dry if regular watering is neglected.

3 Place more seed compost in the seed-tray and strike the surface level with a straight-edged piece of wood. Try to leave the surface of the compost even and flat.

4 Using a piece of wood with a small handle attached to it, firm the surface until it is about 12mm/½in below the rim. Keep the surface of the presser clean to ensure an even surface.

5 Tip the seeds into a folded, V-shaped piece of paper and gently tap the end to encourage them to fall on the compost. Do not sow seeds within 12mm/½in of the edge. Label the box.

6 Some seeds require light to encourage germination, but most need darkness and are covered to three or four times their thickness. Use a fine-mesh sieve to scatter compost.

7 Water the compost by standing the seed-tray in a bowl of clean water. When moisture seeps to the surface, remove and allow to drain. Do not water from overhead, as it scatters the seeds.

8 The seed-tray needs to be covered to prevent the surface of the seed compost drying, as well as maintaining a high temperature. Domed, plastic covers are convenient.

9 An alternative to a plastic cover is a sheet of clear glass. However, condensation accumulates on the underside and this must be wiped off every day, the glass then turned upside down.

10 To create a dark environment for dark-loving seeds sown on, or almost on, the seed compost's surface, cover the glass with a sheet of newspaper. Remove when the seeds germinate.

As soon as the seedlings are large enough to handle they must be moved to where they have more space and an increased amount of air and light.

If not transferred (pricked off), they become drawn up, thin and lanky, and eventually unable to support themselves unless assisted by neighbouring seedlings. Additionally, seedlings tightly clustered together are more susceptible to diseases than those with a good circulation of air around them.

WHEN PRICKING OFF SEEDLINGS ...

• don't use potting compost formed from unsterilized garden soil, as it may contain pests and diseases.
• ensure the roots of seedlings are moist before being pricked off.
• hold young seedlings by a leaf – if held by the stems they soon become damaged if squeezed.
• don't put newly pricked-off seedlings in strong sunlight – until roots are established their intake of water is restricted.

PRICKING OFF SEEDLINGS

1 After seeds germinate, remove the covering and allow air to circulate around the seedlings. Continue to water them by standing the seed-tray in a bowl of water. Avoid wetting the leaves.

2 As soon as the seedlings are large enough to handle, transfer them individually into a potting compost in seed-trays. First, water the seed compost, then loosen a cluster with a small fork.

6 After the seedlings are established, slightly lower the temperature and water from below to prevent leaves becoming wet and the onset of diseases. Fresh air is vital for strong growth.

7 When the young plants are sturdy and growing strongly, transfer them into small pots of potting compost. First water, allowing excess to drain, then pot up individually. Avoid damaging roots.

8 Fill a pot's base with potting compost, so that when potted the plant will be slightly lower than before. This allows for subsequent settlement of compost when watered after potting is completed.

9 Gently hold each plant by its stem and trickle potting compost around the roots. Take care not to squeeze the stem – young plants are easily damaged and subsequently may not recover.

3 *Place the seedlings on damp newspaper. Use a small dibber to make holes, keeping the outer row* 12mm/½in *from the edge, as this is where the potting compost first dries if watering is neglected.*

4 *Hold each seedling by a leaf, not its stem. Position each seedling at about the same depth as before, then gently lever potting compost against the roots, but taking care not to crush them.*

5 *When the box is full of seedlings, gently tap the edges to level the loose surface. Water the seedlings from above to settle potting compost around their roots. Allow excess water to drain from the compost.*

10 *Use the tips of fingers to firm potting compost over and around the roots. Water plants from above to settle it around them, then place in gentle warmth until established.*

11 *As soon as new growth appears, lower the temperature* *and space the pots apart so that the leaves do not touch. Keep the potting* *compost moist, but not continually saturated with water.*

Propagation: Dividing Plants

This is perhaps the easiest way to increase plants. Eventually, many houseplants become congested, the pot packed with stems and roots. Many plants that eventually grow very large can be continually repotted into larger pots, but some become congested and are better removed from their pots, divided into small pieces and repotted.

Houseplants mainly grown for their attractive foliage are best divided in spring. Some flowering types with a perennial nature are also increased in this way, as soon as their flowers fade but preferably in spring. Flowering plants that finish flowering in autumn are best divided in spring. Division in spring enables young plants to become established during summer, while growing strongly.

Congested houseplants usually have developed from one plant, originally central in the pot. Therefore, when dividing plants inspect the centres and if old discard them.

Plants suitable for division include ...
- *Aspidistra elatior*
Aspidistra
- *Calathea makoyana*
Peacock Plant
- *Chlorophytum comosum*
Spider Plant
- *Ctenanthe oppenheimiana tricolor*
Never Never Plant
- *Cyperus alternifolius*
Umbrella Grass
- Ferns – Many can be divided
- *Hedera helix*
Common Ivy
- *Fittonia argyroneura*
Silver Net Leaf
- *Maranta leuconeura*
Prayer Plant
- *Nertera depressa*
Bead Plant
- Palms – many can be divided
- *Saintpaulia ionantha*
African Violet
- *Sansevieria trifaciata*
Mother-in-Law Plant
- *Soleirolia soleirolii*
Mind Your Own Business
- *Spathiphyllum wallisii*
Peace Lily

DIVIDING A PEACE LILY

1 This congested Peace Lily (Spathiphyllum wallisii) is best divided in spring. Remove the soil-ball from the pot by inverting the plant and tapping the rim on the edge of a firm surface.

2 Evidence that division is needed is indicated by a mat of roots around the root-ball. A mass of white roots indicates that the plant is healthy and growing strongly.

DIVIDING A MOTHER-IN-LAW'S TONGUE

1 The yellow-edged form Sansevieria trifasciata 'Laurentii' must be increased by division if the yellow edge is to be perpetuated. Gently pull the root-ball and stems into several pieces.

2 Select a clean pot and place potting compost in its base. Adjust its level so that when repotted the young plant is at the same level as it was previously. Spread out the roots.

3 Ensure the plant is in the centre of the pot and firm potting compost around the roots. Leave a 12mm/½in gap between the potting compost and the pot's rim.

3 *Using fingers, tease and pull apart the root-ball into several substantially-sized pieces. It may be necessary to cut some roots, but never use a knife to slice through a plant.*

4 *Hold a young plant in the centre of a clean pot and trickle fresh potting compost around the roots. Firm the potting compost and ensure the plant is at the same depth as before.*

5 *Water the plants from above and place in gentle warmth. It may be necessary to shade plants from strong sunlight until roots are established and absorbing water. Do not water the plant until the compost has started to dry.*

DIVIDING AFRICAN VIOLETS

4 *It is possible to split a mother plant into several pieces, but take care not to damage the roots. Place the plants in light shade until the roots are established and absorbing water.*

1 *African Violets (Saintpaulia ionantha) that become congested can be increased by division, preferably in spring or early summer. Remove the pot by tapping the rim on a firm surface.*

2 *Gently pull apart the root-ball so that it forms several individual plants. Do not cut with a knife. Do not damage the roots, as this retards the establishment of young plants.*

3 *Pot up each young plant into a clean pot and potting compost. Allow the roots to spread out, then firm with your fingers. Do not excessively compress the potting compost.*

Layering is an easy though not rapid way to increase many climbing and trailing houseplants with flexible stems. Long stems are secured with small pieces of wire into pots of potting compost. When roots form at the position where the shoot is pegged into the soil, it is severed from the parent plant.

Late spring and early summer are the best times to layer plants, while they are growing strongly.

Houseplants to layer
- *Cissus antarctica*
Kangaroo Vine
- *Epipremnum pinnatum*
Devil's Ivy
- *Hedera canariensis* 'Variegata'
Canary Island Ivy
- *Hedera helix* (many variegated forms)
Common Ivy
- *Philodendron scandens*
Sweetheart Plant
- *Plectranthus coleoides marginatus*
Swedish Ivy
- *Rhoicissus rhombifolia*
Grape Ivy

LAYERING AN IVY

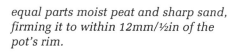

1 Water the mother plant to ensure the stems are turgid and not wilting. Prepare a pot by filling it with equal parts moist peat and sharp sand, firming it to within 12mm/½in of the pot's rim.

2 Bend the stem near to a leaf-joint and 10-15cm/4-6in from its tip. This constricts – but does not sever – the stem, so that the flow of sap is restricted. Roots will form at this point.

3 Use a small piece of U-shaped wire to pin the shoot in the potting compost. Firm it around the bend, then water from above. Place both the mother plant and the layer in a plastic tray. It is then easy to move them.

4 When rooted, young roots can be seen growing from the bend, together with fresh shoots from the shoot's tip. Use a knife or sharp scissors to sever the layer from the mother plant.

2 *Lower a stem to the potting compost, press it about 2.5cm/1in deep and use a bent piece of wire to* secure it into the potting compost. Water the plant to settle the compost around the stem.

1 *If the plant is growing as a climber, release and lower a shoot. Ensure the potting compost in the mother* plant's pot is moist, and fill a small pot with equal parts moist peat and sharp sand.

3 *When young shoots develop from the tip of the stem, use a sharp knife, scissors or secateurs to sever it* from the parent. To tidy up the plant, cut the shoot back to its source.

Air layering is a form of increasing plants practised in India and China from early times to encourage shoots and stems to develop roots. Early methods were known as Gootee-layering and Marcottage and used to increase trees and shrubs with stems that could not be lowered and pegged into soil at ground-level. Nowadays, a similar technique known as air-layering is used to increase plants in greenhouses and the home, although by no means is it restricted to indoor plants.

Large, woody houseplants such as Rubber Plants (*Ficus elastica*) that have become unsightly through the loss of leaves at the lower ends of their stems can be encouraged to develop roots just below the lowest leaf. In this way, a new and attractive plant can be created. Air-layering is best carried out in spring or early summer.

Plants to air-layer
- *Dieffenbachia*
Dumb Cane
- *Dracaena*
- *Ficus elastica*
Rubber Plant
- *Monstera deliciosa*
Swiss Cheese Plant

1 Choose a healthy plant – free from pests, diseases and physiological damage – but bare of leaves at the bottom of its stem. The top 45cm/1½ft of the plant should have leaves.

2 Use a sharp knife to make an upward-slanting cut, two-thirds through the stem and 7.5-10cm/3-4in below the lowest leaf. Take care that the top of the plant does not bend over.

3 Use a matchstick to keep the cut surfaces open. At this stage, the wound will exude latex (sap) which is best wiped away with a damp cloth. Trim off the ends of long matches.

8 Keep the potting compost in the plant's pot moist but not continually saturated, and within six to eight weeks roots will develop and can be seen through the polythene.

9 Hold the top of the plant and, with sharp secateurs, sever the stem immediately below the peat. Gently remove the polythene. Peat will fall away, some will remain around the roots.

10 Before the roots become dry and thereby damaged, pot up the plant into potting compost. Take care not to damage the roots, or to constrict them in a very small pot.

11 Trickle potting compost around the roots. Lifting the plant up several times helps potting compost to trickle between roots. Until established, stake the plant.

4 *Use a small brush to coat the cut surfaces with hormone rooting-powder. This encourages the rapid formation of roots. Push the powder well inside the cut.*

5 *Wind a piece of clear polythene film, about 30cm/12in long by 23cm/9in wide, around the stem. Use string to tie the bottom around the stem, a few inches below the cut.*

6 *Fill the tube formed by the polythene film with moist peat or sphagnum moss, pushing it firmly but not solidly around the cut stem. Fill to within 7.5cm/3in of the tube's top.*

7 *Use strong string to tie the top of the polythene tube to the stem, in the same way as previously used at the base. Take care not to damage the stem by tying them too tightly.*

1 *Do not throw away the old plant: cut the stem back to slightly above a bud. Place the plant in gentle warmth, keep the compost moist and within a few weeks several young shoots will develop.*

2 *A cluster of stems usually develops at the plant's base. If a bushy plant is desired leave them intact, but for a single-stemmed plant remove all but the largest and strongest.*

Propagation: Runners and Plantlets

Encouraging runners and plantlets to form roots is an interesting and easy method to increase plants. A few houseplants, such as the Spider Plant (*Chlorophytum comosum*) develop trailing stems with plantlets at their tips which when pegged into potting compost develop roots.

A few plants have small plantlets along the surfaces of their leaves – or at their ends – that can be removed and encouraged to form roots.

INCREASING A CHANDELIER PLANT

*1 The Chandelier Plant (*Kalanchoe tubiflora, *but earlier known as* Bryophyllum tubiflorum*), develops clusters of small plantlets at the ends of its tubular, succulent leaves.*

2 With age, the plantlets become large and develop hair-like roots that help to secure them in the potting compost. In Nature, they fall and soon establish themselves on damp soil.

3 Gently pull off several plantlets, taking care not to damage leaves. So that the mother plant retains an attractive appearance, remove plantlets from all over it, not just from one place.

INCREASING A MEXICAN HAT

*1 The Mexican Hat (*Kalanchoe daigremontiana, *but earlier known as* Bryophyllum daigremontianum), develops plantlets around the edges of its thick, succulent, somewhat hat-shaped leaves.*

2 Individual plantlets grow and mature until, in Nature, they fall off on to surrounding soil. If this is moist, they soon develop roots and produce clusters of plants.

3 Gently pull off large and mature plantlets, taking care not to remove them from just one leaf as this will spoil the mother plant's overall appearance.

4 Place the plantlets on the surface of potting compost in a 7.5cm/3in wide pot. Plantlets can be scattered on the surface, but when spaced apart each is in less competition with its neighbour.

5 When rooted and growing strongly, pot up the young plants individually into 7.5cm/3in wide pots. Unlike Kalanchoe tubiflora, this plant is best grown singly, not in clusters.

4 Scatter plantlets on the surface of damp potting compost. They invariably fall in clusters and therefore need to be spaced by manipulating them with the tip of a knife or pencil.

5 Gently press plantlets into the potting compost. Water by standing the pot in a tray of water until moisture seeps to the top, then allow to drain. Place in gentle warmth.

6 Keep moist and when the plantlets are rooted and have developed shoots, gently transplant into larger pots, either singly or three to a 7.5cm/3in wide pot. When established, place on a windowsill.

INCREASING A SPIDER PLANT

1 Chlorophytum comosum *develops long, trailing and arching stems with small plantlets at their ends. When pegged into pots of potting compost placed around the mother plant they develop roots.*

2 Use small pieces of bent wire to secure the plantlets into the potting compost. Water and place in gentle warmth. Placing the mother plant and plantlets in a tray helps when moving them.

3 When young shoots start to develop from the plantlets, sever the shoots from the parent plant and move them into a lightly shaded position until growing strongly. Keep the potting compost moist.

Many houseplants can be increased from stem-tip cuttings, each formed from a piece of stem, several leaves and a terminal shoot. They are usually 7.5-13cm/3-5in long and, if possible, taken from the outer area of the parent plant, where they would have been in good light and growing healthily and strongly. Spindly and weak shoots are not suitable as cuttings. Additionally, ensure that the mother plant is turgid – wilting plants never produce good cuttings.

Cuttings need a moisture-retentive yet well aerated potting compost to encourage rapid rooting, such as equal parts moist peat and sharp sand.

Mother plants

Sometimes is it impossible to take cuttings from a plant without spoiling its appearance. Also, some plants grown indoors do not produce young shoots that can be used as cuttings.

In greenhouses and conservatories it is often possible to grow plants in out-of-

TAKING STEM-TIP CUTTINGS

1 Use a sharp knife to cut a strong and healthy shoot from a mother plant, severing it just above a leaf-joint. Do not leave short spurs, as they are unsightly and encourage the onset of diseases and decay.

3 Dip the cutting's base in hormone rooting-powder. Use a small dibber to form a hole into which the stem is inserted 18-25mm/¾-1in. Do not bury the lower leaves, as this encourages rotting.

4 Firm compost around the cutting's base, water from above, insert short split-canes in the potting compost and cover with a plastic bag. Secure its base around the pot with an elastic-band.

2 Trim the cutting's base to just below a leaf-joint, at the same time cutting off lower leaves close to the stem. Some cuttings have two leaves at each leaf-joint, others just one.

the-way positions, specifically to create young shoots that can be used as cuttings. The Zebra Plant (*Aphelandra squarrosa*), Rose of China (*Hibiscus rosa-sinensis*) and the Lollipop Plant (*Pachystachys lutea*) are frequently cut back in spring or after flowers fade, young shoots then growing from leaf-joints. These are subsequently used as cuttings.

Heel-cuttings
Some plants grown in greenhouses, conservatories and indoors have a slightly woody nature. These include the Rose of China (*Hibiscus rosa-sinensis*). Young shoots when 7.5-10cm/3-4in long are gently pulled from the stem, so that a small piece of woody stem (a heel) is attached to its base. Ragged edges are trimmed before dipping the end in hormone rooting powder and inserting in equal parts moist peat and sharp sand.

Plectranthus coleoides Marginatus

Stem cuttings resemble stem-tip cuttings, but without a tip. It's an excellent way to increase plants with long, trailing stems. Additionally, it enables several cuttings to be created from a shoot, rather than just one as with stem-tip cuttings.

Spring and early summer are the best times to take and root these cuttings, but if you have a propagation frame with soil-warming cables it is possible to take them throughout the year. However, by taking them in spring it ensures that cuttings are rooted and young plants established by the onset of winter.

Ivies – especially the small-leaved types – are increased in this way.

INCREASING AN IVY

1 Cut a long, young shoot from a parent plant. Do not use old and tough shoots. It is better to cut off an entire shoot, rather than to leave short, unsightly spurs on the mother plant, that may encourage diseases.

4 Gently water the potting compost to settle it around the cuttings, and insert four short split-canes into the compost. Place a plastic bag over the canes and hold it firm with a rubber band.

5 Place in gentle warmth and light shade. When young shoots develop from the leaf-joints, check that roots have formed. Remove the plastic bag and allow the cuttings plenty of fresh air.

2 Use a sharp knife to cut the shoot into several cuttings – ragged cuts do not heal quickly and produce roots.

Cut slightly above each leaf-joint, leaving a piece of stem 36mm/1½in long.

3 Use a small dibber (or pencil) to insert cuttings 18-30mm/¾-1¼in into equal parts moist peat and sharp

sand. Firm each cutting – do not insert closer than 18mm/¾in to the pot's edge, as this is where compost first becomes dry.

6 Pot up rooted cuttings into pots of potting compost. Put either one, three or five cuttings in each pot – the higher the number of cuttings in a pot, the quicker a bushy plant is created.

Propagation: Leaf-Petiole Cuttings

Each cutting is formed of a leaf together with the short stem (petiole) attaching it to the plant. The most popular plant raised in this way is *Saintpaulia ionantha*.

INCREASING AFRICAN VIOLETS
These are extremely popular plants for the home, easy to grow and very colourful throughout most of the year, and increased by rooting leaf stalks.

1 In spring and early summer select a healthy plant. Use a sharp knife to cut off leaves with their leaf-stalks intact – avoid leaving short stumps. Take care not to spoil the plant's shape.

2 Use a sharp knife to trim back the stems to about 36mm/1½in long. Stems are easily bruised and damaged, so take great care when handling and cutting them. Hold each cutting by its leaf.

AFRICAN VIOLETS ROOTED IN WATER

1 Instead of inserting leaf-stems in compost, they can also be suspended in water. First, fill a glass bottle to within 18mm/¾in of its top. Short milk bottles are ideal for this purpose.

2 Wrap a piece of paper over the top and secure with string or an elastic band. Gently pierce the paper with a sharp-pointed knife. Do not make the hole too large, as the stem must fit snugly.

3 Push the leaf-stem through the hole so that the lower 6-12mm/¼-½in is in the water. Place in gentle warmth and slight shade. Occasionally check the water to ensure the stem's base is covered.

3 Dip the end of each stem into a hormone rooting powder. This powder is often combined with a fungicide that helps to prevent diseases attacking the cuttings before they develop roots.

4 Insert the stem of each leaf about 2.5cm/1in into a mixture of equal parts moist peat and sharp sand. Firm the compost around the stems. When small shoots appear, pot up into potting compost.

4 When roots have developed from the cut end, pot up the cutting into a potting compost. Use a small pot, as African Violets do not grow well when they have a vast amount of potting compost.

Propagation: Whole Leaf Cuttings

Leaves of some houseplants, such as large-leaved begonias, can be encouraged to form roots along their undersides, with shoots developing from the upper surfaces. When established, these are separated and potted into small pots of potting compost.

Plants to increase by whole-leaf cuttings
- *Begonia rex*
Rex Begonia
- *Begonia masoniana*
Iron Cross Begonia
- *Streptocarpus hybridus*
Cape Primrose

QUICK TIPS

Gentle warmth is better than a high temperature. Indeed, a shaded north-facing windowsill in summer often encourages better rooting than a high temperature in a greenhouse.

INCREASING A LARGE-LEAVED BEGONIA

1 Select a healthy leaf – free from pests and diseases – and sever the stem close to the plant's base. Do not leave a short piece of stem at the base, as it encourages the onset of decay and diseases.

2 Turn the leaf upside down and, with a sharp knife, sever the stem close to the leaf. Do not use old leaves that are stiff and brittle. Roots form more rapidly on young leaves.

5 An alternative way to keep the leaf in contact with the potting compost is to use small U-shaped pieces of wire. Insert them so that they are astride the main and secondary veins.

6 Place the plastic container in a bowl shallowly filled with water until moisture appears on the surface of the potting compost. Remove, allow the compost to drain and cover with a transparent lid.

3 *Use a sharp knife or razor blade to cut across the veins on the underside of a leaf, about 18-25mm/¾-* 1in apart. Sever both the main and secondary veins. Do not cut through the complete leaf.

4 *Place the leaf vein-side downwards and press firmly so that it is in close contact with the potting compost* in a plastic seed-tray. Hold the leaf in position by placing a few small stones on top.

7 *Place in gentle warmth. Keep the potting compost moist and occasionally wipe condensation from* the inside of the lid. Young plants eventually grow from the cut surfaces. Remove the lid.

8 *When established, the young plants are transferred to small pots of potting compost. Don't constrict the* roots, and ensure each plant's base is not buried, as this encourages decay and diseases.

Large-leaved begonias can be increased by cutting their leaves into triangles and inserting them in compost. Young and healthy leaves root faster than old ones, and discard those that are damaged or infected by pests or diseases.

A variation on leaf-triangles is leaf-squares (see pages 52/53). The triangles tend to be longer than the squares and therefore can be inserted deeper into the potting compost and given a firmer base. However, more leaf-squares can be cut from a similarly-sized leaf.

Suitable plants
• *Begonia masoniana*
Iron Cross Begonia
• *Begonia rex*
Rex Begonia

2 Turn the leaf upside down and cut off the stem, close to its base. Do not take leaves from plants growing in dry compost as they quickly shrivel and do not produce roots. The plant must be turgid.

1 Select a healthy leaf and sever it close to the plant's base. Avoid leaving short spurs. If only a few leaves are needed, cut from opposite sides to avoid creating an imbalanced shape and spoiling the effect.

3 Place the leaf on a flat piece of wood and cut it into triangles. The tip of the triangle should be towards the centre of the leaf. Several cuttings can be taken from one leaf. Always use a sharp knife

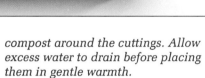

4 Insert the cuttings, pointed-end downwards and to about half their length, in potting compost. Firm the potting compost around them, ensuring they are upright and not touching each other.

5 Lightly water the cuttings from above, using a watering-can with a fine spray. This helps to settle potting compost around the cuttings. Allow excess water to drain before placing them in gentle warmth.

6 Cover with a translucent plastic lid, occasionally removing it to wipe away condensation. Periodically, check the potting compost is moist – water by standing the tray in water. Avoid making the leaves wet.

7 When rooted, carefully lever up plants and pot up individually into small pots of potting compost. Water the compost and place in gentle warmth until established and growing strongly.

Leaf-squares are a popular way to increase large-leaved plants such as some begonias. Healthy, relatively young leaves create the best cuttings; ensure that the potting compost is moist before a leaf is severed. It is essential that a leaf is turgid and full of water — dry leaves never create strong, healthy and fast-rooting cuttings.

Suitable plants
- *Begonia masoniana*
Iron Cross Begonia
- *Begonia rex*
Rex Begonia

1 Sever the leaf-stalk close to the leaf. Turn the leaf upside down and cut strips 30mm/1¼in wide.

Ensure each strip has a main vein along its centre. Several strips can be cut from one leaf.

3 Use a knife blade to form a slit about 12mm/½in deep in the potting compost, into which leaf-

squares can be inserted. The end that was nearest to the leaf-stalk should face downwards.

2 Using a sharp knife or razor blade, cut the strips into squares. Ensure that each piece has several cut veins.

Don't make the squares too small, as they are then slow to root and may decay before roots form.

4 Firm compost around the bases of the leaf-squares, then use a watering-can with a fine spray gently to

water them. Allow excess water to drain and put a transparent cover over them.

5 Place the leaf-squares in gentle warmth. If the surface becomes dry, water by standing the seed-tray in a bowl of water until moisture rises to the surface. Pot up when rooted.

6 Gently remove rooted leaf-cuttings from the seed-tray and pot up individually into small pots of potting compost. Place in gentle warmth until established and growing strongly.

Some plants can be increased by cutting leaves cross-wise and inserting them in well-drained and aerated potting compost.

Plants to increase from cross-sections of leaves
- *Sansevieria trifasciata*
Mother-in-Law's Tongue
- *Sinningia speciosa*
Gloxinia
- *Streptocarpus hybridus*
Cape Primrose

INCREASING CAPE PRIMROSE
Streptocarpus can be increased in late spring and early summer from cross-sections of leaves.

1 Select a pest-and-disease-free mother plant and water the potting compost. Leaves taken from dry plants do not readily develop roots. Choose a healthy leaf and cut sections about 5cm/2in deep.

2 Fill a pot or seedtray with equal parts moist peat and sharp sand, form a narrow slit 18mm/¾in deep and insert the base of the leaf-cutting into it. Firm potting compost around its base.

3 Water and place in a slightly-heated propagation frame – or cover with a plastic lid. It is essential that the leaf is not continually covered in moisture, as it then quickly decays.

INCREASING A MOTHER-IN-LAW'S TONGUE

The ordinary form of *Sansevieria trifasciata* can be increased by cutting leaves into sections. The variety 'Laurentii', which has yellow edges to the leaves, must be increased by division to retain the attractive colouring.

1 Select a healthy plant and remove one or two leaves, cutting them off immediately at their bases. Take care not to spoil the plant's shape by removing too many leaves.

2 Cut each leaf into cross-sections about 5cm/2in deep. Use a sharp knife to cut the leaves – avoid tearing them. Ensure that the cut sections are not turned upside down.

3 Fill a pot or seedtray with equal parts moist peat and sharp sand. Usually the sections can be pushed about 18mm/¾in into the potting compost.

4 Firm potting compost around each cutting's base and gently water from overhead. Subsequently, water by standing the pot in a bowl shallowly filled with water.

Propagation: Cacti and Other Succulents

As well as being increased from seeds, cacti and other succulents are frequently propagated from cuttings. Take cacti cuttings during spring and summer, from plants that are healthy and well watered. However, cuttings taken early in the year root faster than those in late summer, and will be well established by the onset of winter. Kitchen gloves enable excessively spiny types to be handled without the risk of damaging your hands.

ROOTING SUCCULENT LEAVES

Succulents such as some crassulas and echeverias can be increased from whole-leaf cuttings inserted upright in a sandy potting compost. Like most other cuttings, spring and early summer are the best times to take them. The succulent increased here is the Jade Plant (*Crassula argentea*).

1 Use a sharp knife to sever stems. Do not take too many cuttings from one plant – its shape will be spoilt.

Young stems from around the outside of a clump root quicker than central, old ones.

2 Do not immediately insert the cuttings into a rooting compost. Instead, allow their cut surfaces to dry for a few days. This enables them to root faster than if directly inserted.

1 Select a healthy, well watered plant and gently pull off mature and fleshy leaves close to the stem. Avoid leaving short spurs, as these will spoil the mother plant's shape.

3 Use equal parts moist peat and sharp sand. Sprinkle a thin layer of sand on the surface and then use a small dibber to create a hole into which the cutting can be inserted and firmed.

4 Lightly water the potting compost to settle it around each cutting and then place in gentle warmth. In spring and early summer rooting takes a few weeks, but later in the year it is much longer.

4 Firm potting compost around the base of each leaf. Then lightly water and place in gentle warmth, but out of direct sunlight. Place in a propagation frame, or on a shaded window-sill.

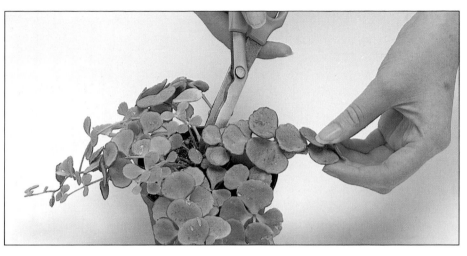

SMALL AND CIRCULAR SUCCULENT LEAVES

Succulent plants with small and relatively flat succulent leaves are easily increased in spring and early summer by pressing the leaves into the surface of well-drained potting compost. Plants that can be increased in this way include *Sedum sieboldii*. There is also an attractive variegated form of this plant.

Allow the cut surfaces to dry for a couple of days before inserting them in well drained and aerated potting compost, formed of equal parts moist peat and grit – with a surface layer of sharp sand.

3 Use a small dibber or knife to form a hole in the potting compost. Insert several cuttings in one pot, ensuring they are not close to the edges – this is where the potting compost first becomes dry.

1 Cut off entire stems, right back to the plant's base – do not leave short spurs. Only remove a few shoots from each plant. If too many are cut off this seriously spoils the plant's shape.

2 Snap off individual leaves from the stems, taking care not to crush or damage them. Allow the cut surfaces to dry for a couple of days before inserting them in the compost.

When young shoots develop from the bases of the leaves, gently pot into a sandy potting compost. Water and place in gentle warmth until the young plants are established and growing strongly.

3 Fill a pot with equal parts moist peat and sharp sand, with a surface layer of sand, and press the leaves into the potting compost. Water lightly and place in gentle warmth in light shade.

Cane cuttings are used to increase several thick-stemmed house-plants, such as yuccas, cordylines, dracaenas and dieffenbachias. These are plants that often lose their lower leaves.

Chopping up stems to form cuttings obviously destroys a plant – especially with yuccas, cordylines and dracaenas – but does eventually create several others. Dieffenbachias, however, usually have several stems and the removal of just one to form cuttings does not destroy the plant. Spring and early summer are the best times to take and root these cuttings.

There are two types of cane cuttings: those laid horizontally on the potting compost, and ones that are inserted vertically.

HORIZONTAL CANE CUTTINGS

Dieffenbachias, dracaenas and cordylines can be increased in this way.

1 Sever a strong and healthy stem at its base, trying not to spoil the plant's shape. However, sometimes it is better to use the entire plant as cuttings than to nurse the unsightly remains.

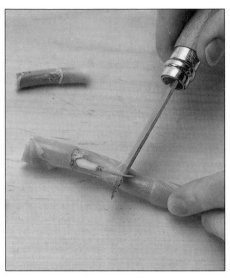

2 Use a sharp knife to cut the stems into 5-7.5cm/2-3in lengths, each having at least one strong and healthy bud. These buds grow from the old leaf-joints (nodes).

VERTICAL CANE CUTTINGS

Yuccas, as well as dracaenas which have lost their lower leaves and have stiff, woody stems, can be increased by inserting cuttings vertically into potting compost.

These are frequently known as Ti-log cuttings, although often it is *Dracaena terminalis* – correctly known as *Cordyline fruticosa* and widely sold as *C. terminalis* – that is widely called the Ti Plant. It is also known as the Lucky Plant and Good Luck Plant. There is often confusion between *dracaenas* and *cordylines*: in general, the roots of dracaenas when cut are orange, while those of cordylines are white.

Ti-log cuttings can be bought from garden centres. Frequently, however, they are bought during holidays abroad. Cuttings from Brazil are sold as Lucky Plants and usually have their ends sealed with paraffin wax to reduce the rate at which they become dry. The top of each cane is indicated by a different coloured wax from that used at the base. This is to ensure that when potted the cane is not inserted the wrong way up – the instructions on the packaging indicates the colour coding.

3 Fill and firm a pot with equal parts moist peat and sharp sand. Press each cutting – the bud facing upwards – to half its thickness in the compost, and secure with pieces of bent wire. Do not squash the stems.

4 Water lightly, allow to drain and insert small pieces of split cane around the pot's edge. Place a plastic bag over the pot. Alternatively, use a plastic dome. Place in gentle warmth.

TI CUTTINGS IN WATER

As well as being grown in potting compost, Ti-log cuttings can be grown in water. Stand each cutting in a glass jar containing about 2.5cm/1in of clean water. Place in 8°C/46°F, changing the water every four or five days. After three or four weeks dormant buds start to grow.

Cuttings can be left in the water. Top up with water and a few drops of liquid fertilizer every six weeks in summer. However, for long-term success, grow Ti-cuttings in compost, where they will be regularly provided with water and nutrients. Also, the compost and pot create a firm base for the plant that eventually may grow more than 1.5m/5ft high and 90cm/3ft wide. Loam-based compost provides a much firmer base than those mainly created from peat.

1 *Cut or scrape away wax from the lower end, but leave the wax on the top-end intact. This wax helps to prevent the loss of moisture from the cutting before it forms roots.*

2 *The cutting is inserted with the bare end downwards into the compost, the top still covered with wax. Do not use a large pot, as this may create a large amount of cold, wet compost.*

3 *Fill a 7.5-10cm/3-4in wide pot with equal parts moist peat and sharp sand. It is essential that it is well drained and aerated. Waterlogged compost encourages the cuttings to decay and rot..*

4 *Insert the cutting, then firm the potting compost around it. The lower 36-50mm/1½-2in should be buried in the compost. Water the compost and allow excess to drain.*

5 *To encourage rapid rooting, place the pot and cutting in an opaque bag and place in gentle warmth. Inspect the compost every ten days to ensure it has not become dry. When shoots appear, remove the bag and slowly acclimatize the plant to a lower temperature and less humidity. When the pot is full of roots, transfer it to a larger pot.*

Bulbs and corms are miracles of the plant world. They are storehouses of flower power, remaining dormant for long periods then bursting into growth and colour after being given a cold period followed by gentle warmth. In Nature, most bulbs burst into flower in spring, after the coldness of winter. But if they are exposed to cool periods in autumn and early winter, then given warmth, early flowering is encouraged. Also, some bulbs are specially treated by bulb specialists to encourage extra early flowering. These are known as 'specially-prepared' bulbs.

HYACINTHS

Few bulbous plants are as stately – or sweetly-scented – as hyacinths. Never mix varieties in the same bowl, as they seldom flower at the same. Indeed, hyacinths are sometimes grown individually and at flowering time those at the same stage of development put into one bowl. Normally, bulbs of Dutch hyacinths are planted from late summer to early autumn for flowering from mid winter to early spring. 'Specially-prepared' bulbs ensure flowers at Christmas. The Roman hyacinths, with dainty flowers on slender stems, are planted in late summer for flowering during early and late winter.

1 Plant healthy, equally-sized bulbs of the same variety in a clean, 18-23cm/7-9in wide, bulb bowl. Half fill with damp bulb-fibre or potting compost. Put one bulb in the centre.

2 Place other bulbs around the central one, spacing them 12mm/½in apart. When planted, the noses of the bulbs must be above the surface of the potting compost.

3 Use your fingers to pack bulb-fibre or potting compost firmly – but not rammed – around the bulbs. When completed, the potting mixture should be 12mm/½in below the pot's rim.

4 Water thoroughly with a fine-rosed watering-can, allowing excess to drain. Place the pot in a cool, dark, vermin-proof place to encourage the development of roots.

5 Put the pot in a black polythene bag and place in a cool cellar or shed. Or put outside on a firm surface, *against a north-facing wall, and cover with 20cm/8in of moist peat, then black polythene.*

6 When the roots are well developed and the shoots 5-7.5cm/2-3in above the compost, move the pot to a *cool position indoors. Keep the potting compost moist. Do not exceed 10°C/50°F.*

HYACINTHS IN BULB-GLASS

An unusual and eye-catching way to grow hyacinths for winter is in bulb-glasses (modern ones are made of plastic). They resemble hour-glasses, the upper part holding a bulb and the lower half acting as a water reservoir.

1 In late summer, fill a bulb-glass with clean water so that when a bulb is placed on top its base is just covered. Do not overfill with water, as the base of the bulb will then rot.

Place in a cool, dark, frost-free cellar or garage until roots have grown about 10cm/4in long and the shoots are 2.5cm/1in out of the neck of the bulb. Regularly check the water level.

2 When the shoots and roots have developed, move the bulb-glass into a cool position indoors. Slowly increase the temperature to 18°C/64°F. Keep the water level with the bulb's base.

As well as growing hyacinths indoors in bowls and bulb-glasses, they also create an exciting Christmas feature in glass bowls, 20-23cm/8-9in wide and 13-15cm/5-6in deep.

Half fill the bowl in early autumn with clean, 6mm/¼in gravel chippings. Place five bulbs – one in the centre and the rest surrounding it – on the chippings, so that their noses will be above the surface of the gravel, itself 12mm/½in below the bowl's rim.

Fill the bottom of the bowl with water, so that its surface rests 12mm/½in below the bases of the bulbs. Place the bowl in a dark place, at 5-10°C/41-50°F. Periodically, check the level of the water.

When the tops of the bulbs are 7.5cm/3in above the surface of the gravel, move the bowl indoors. Maintain the level of the water fractionally below the bulbs .

AFTER FLOWERING INDOORS ...

Many bulbs that flower indoors can later be planted in a garden. These include daffodils, tulips, hyacinths and crocuses. Bulbs grown indoors in potting compost usually flower the following year, whereas those in bulb-fibre often take a year or more to recover. However, to most people bulb-fibre is cleaner and easier to use. As flowers fade, remove them and place the container in a cool, light, frost-free place. Do not allow the potting compost to become dry. During spring, remove the bulbs and potting compost and plant in a sheltered position in the garden. They can be used to fill gaps between shrubs, or to form a naturalized garden. They cannot again be forced for flowering indoors.

DAFFODILS

Daffodils are types of *Narcissus*, distinguished by having large central tubes, known as trumpets, at least as long as one of the petals. All others are broadly known as narcissi. Both types are grown in pots for flowering indoors. Early flowering is encouraged by planting 'specially-prepared' bulbs.

1 In late summer, pot up healthy bulbs in clean, well-drained, 18-23cm/7-9in wide pots containing damp bulb-fibre or potting compost. Half fill the bowl with one of these potting mixtures.

2 Place the bulbs close together, with their noses about level with the container's rim. This will ensure that they are at about the correct height after the potting mixture has been added.

3 Pack bulb-fibre or potting compost around each bulb, gently working it between them. Eventually, the surface of the potting mixture should be 12mm/½in below the container's rim.

4 Thoroughly water the potting mixture to settle it around each bulb. To encourage the development of roots the pot must be placed in a cool, dark, vermin-proof place. Inspect the pots regularly.

5 Put the pot in a black polythene bag and place in a cool cellar or shed. Or put outside on a firm surface, against a north-facing wall, and cover with 20cm/8in of moist peat, then black polythene.

6 Leave the bulbs for 12 to 15 weeks, until shoots are 10cm/4in high. Then take indoors, slowly increasing the temperature from 7°C/45°F to 15°C/60°F. Keep the potting mixture moist.

TULIPS

Several tulips are suitable for forcing to flower in spring, including 'Early Single' and 'Early Double' types. Plant in late summer or early autumn for flowering from mid winter to mid spring.

For early flowering plant 'specially-prepared' bulbs as soon as they are available in late summer.

1 In late summer place bulbs close together and deep enough so that their noses will be below the surface of the potting mixture, itself 12mm/½in below the container's rim.

2 Use your fingers to spread and firm the potting mixture between and over the bulbs. Unlike hyacinths and daffodils, tulip bulbs must be covered with the potting mixture.

3 Thoroughly water the potting mixture. To encourage root development, place the container in a cool, dark, vermin-proof area. Put the pot in a black polythene bag and place in a cool cellar or shed. Or put outside and cover with 20cm/8in of moist peat, then black polythene.

4 Between 14 and 16 weeks later (less for 'specially prepared' bulbs) shoots will be about 5cm/2in high. Move indoors to 45-50°C/7-10°F. When the foliage is 10cm/4in high gradually increase to 18°C/64°F. Water regularly to keep the potting compost or bulb-fibre moist.

CROCUSES FOR SPRING

Brightly-faced crocuses (*Crocus chrysanthus*) flower outdoors in late winter and spring. They can also be encouraged to flower indoors, slightly earlier. However, they cannot be forced in the same way as daffodils and tulips – high temperatures soon kill them.

The normal *Crocus chrysanthus* types are better for growing indoors than the large-flowered hybrids. Handle the corms with care – avoid snapping off young shoots.

Pot up in late summer for flowering indoors in late winter. Use shallow pots, as well as special crocus bowls with holes in their sides.

1 In late summer, pot up top-sized corms, using moist bulb-fibre or gritty potting compost. Space the corms 18mm/¾in apart and 5cm/2in deep. Also, position some to grow out through the holes in the sides of the pot. Lightly water the compost.

Either place the pot in a black polythene bag, and place in a vermin-proof cellar, shed or garage, or position outside on a firm, well-drained surface against a north-facing wall. Cover with 10cm/4in of moist peat, then with black polythene. Regularly check that the potting compost is moist.

2 When shoots are about 2.5cm/ 1in high, move the pot indoors into a cool position. Keep the potting compost moist and do not expose to high temperatures, as this soon causes them to fail.

IIIPPEASTRUMS

Often known as Amaryllis and related to the bulbous Belladonna Lily (*Amaryllis belladonna*, a tender garden bulb), Hippeastrums create large, funnel-shaped flowers at the tops of stiff stems. Bulbs planted in late summer and early autumn flower in late winter and spring. However, specially-prepared bulbs if planted in autumn will flower at Christmas and the New Year. Additionally, there are types that can be planted in early spring for flowering in summer and autumn.

1 Pot up bulbs individually into 13-15cm/5-6in wide pots. Use potting compost and leave half of the bulb exposed. Water the potting compost thoroughly and place in 13-16°C/55-61°F.

2 Keep the compost lightly moist until shoots appear, then increase the frequency of watering. When the bulb is growing strongly, feed at weekly intervals with a weak liquid fertilizer. After the flowers fade, continue to water and apply a weekly feed until leaves become yellow. Then, stop feeding and watering and allow the bulb – still in its pot – to dry. Repot the bulb every year, giving it fresh potting compost.

Planting a Bottle Garden

Many small houseplants can be grown in a wide range of glass containers, mainly carboys but also ornate and unusually-shaped bottles and glass domes.

OPEN OR CLOSED CONTAINERS?

Traditionally, bottle gardens once planted were 'stoppered' and the moisture and air inside recycled by the plants. In recent years, however, many other containers have been used, some left open to the air.

With 'stoppered' containers it is essential to achieve the correct degree of moisture in the compost – the critical factor when creating a bottle garden. After planting, wait a day before putting on the stopper to allow excess moisture to escape. If, after the top is put on, the inside becomes misted but clears by midday, the moisture content is correct and it can be left closed. However, if vast amounts of moisture collects on the inside of the glass, there is too much water and the top must be left off for a couple of days. Conversely, if after planting, watering and being stoppered no moisture appears on the glass, the compost is too dry and needs light watering.

Suitable plants

There are many plants to choose from, for both 'stoppered' and 'unstoppered' containers. Flowering plants, as well as large, fast-growing, hairy-surfaced or soft-leaved types are unsuitable for stoppered containers.
- *Acorus gramineus* 'Variegatus' (unstoppered)
- *Adiantum capillus-veneris* (stoppered or unstoppered)
- *Adiantum raddianum* (stoppered or unstoppered)
- *Asplenium nidus* (stoppered or unstoppered)
- *Asplenium trichomanes* (stoppered or unstoppered)
- *Blechnum penna-marina* (stoppered or unstoppered)
- *Cryptanthus acaulis* (stoppered or unstoppered)

PLANTING A CARBOY

1 Form a 2.5cm/1in thick layer of gravel chippings, then a thin layer of charcoal, in the base. Use a funnel formed of cardboard to add a 5cm/2in thick layer of potting compost.

- *Cryptanthus zonatus* (stoppered or unstoppered)
- *Cyrtomium falcatum* (unstoppered)
- *Ficus pumila* (stoppered or unstoppered)
- *Fittonia verschaffeltii* 'Argyroneura Nana' (unstoppered)
- *Hedera helix* (stoppered or unstoppered)
- *Pellaea rotundifolia* (stoppered or unstoppered)
- *Peperomia caperata* (unstoppered)
- *Peperomia magnoliifolia* 'Variegata' (stoppered or unstoppered)
- *Pilea cadierei* 'Nana' (unstoppered)
- *Pilea involucrata* (unstoppered)
- *Pteris cretica* 'Albolineata' (stoppered and unstoppered)
- Sansevieria trifasciata 'Hahnii' (unstoppered)
- *Selaginella kraussiana* 'Aurea' (stoppered and unstoppered)
- *Soleirolia soleirolii* (stoppered or unstoppered)

2 Remove plants from their pots and tease out roots. Start planting from the centre outwards. If the opening is narrow, use spoons and forks tied to short canes to manipulate them.

3 To make the surface of the potting compost more attractive, sprinkle an even layer of either well-washed shingle or expanded clay particles over it. Do not cover the plants.

4 Lightly water the compost by
 dribbling water down the inside of
the glass. This is better than splashing
water over the plants, which may then
encourage the onset of decay in some
plants.

5 As plants grow, invasive ones may
 need trimming to prevent the
container becoming like a jungle. Use
sharp scissors, or a razor-blade
attached to a cane, to cut back long
stems.

Also known as terrariums, these are glass cases that, like carboys and other enclosed glass containers, create a humid atmosphere. Early ones resembled rectangular fish tanks, but recent designs are more ornate and in a variety of sizes and interesting shapes.

Leaded-glass terrariums are very attractive and when filled with plants create eye-catching features. Planting and caring for them is easier than when in a carboy, and for this reason the range of suitable plants is wider.

Terraria plants
As well as those plants recommended for bottle gardens (see pages 66 and 67), the following are suitable.
• *Begonia* 'Tiger'
• *Calathea makoyana*
• *Chamaedorea elegans*
• *Hypocyrta glabra*
• *Hypoestes phyllostachya*
• *Microcoelum weddelianum*

Shapely terraria
Terraria are available in a wide range of sizes and shapes. They are ideal for decorating warm rooms where the light is filtered and gentle.

Shapes range from square and round-ended greenhouses to pagodas. Some have removable roofs, enabling easy planting and care of the plants, while others have removable side panels.

Avoid terraria with stained or highly-embellished glass, as it is then difficult to see the plants.

PLANTING A TERRARIUM

1 Mark out the area of the terrarium on a piece of card or paper, then arrange the plants on it until a pleasing combination is formed. Use one or two tall plants to create variations in height in the terrarium.

4 Starting at one end, make a depression in the potting compost and set the plant in position, firming soil around it. It is usually necessary first to tease and spread out the plant's roots.

5 While setting the plants in position it is likely that the inside of the glass will become dirty. This can be removed by tying a piece of sponge to a small cane, then wiping the glass with a dry cloth.

2 *Before planting, ensure the plants are clean. Wipe smooth-leaved plants with a damp cloth, while hairy-* 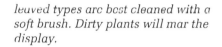 *leaved types are best cleaned with a soft brush. Dirty plants will mar the display.*

3 *Spread a 18mm/¾in layer of washed gravel over the terrarium's base, then a thin layer of charcoal and 5cm/2in of loam-based potting compost. Ensure the compost is damp, but not soaked in water.*

6 *Mist-spray smooth-leaved plants and lightly dampen the surface of the potting compost. Avoid swamping it with water. Close all apertures and leave the terrarium for a few days. Avoid placing it in draughts.*

7 *If vast amounts of condensation build up on the inside of the glass, it indicates that the potting compost is too wet. Leave an aperture open for a day to remove excess moisture.*

Displaying houseplants in indoor hanging-baskets needs care and planning. They attractively fill vertical space but can be difficult to water and look after. Also, they need firm securing points. Although similar to outdoor hanging-baskets, indoor types must be fitted with drip trays to ensure excess water does not fall on carpets. In conservatories with tiled floors this is not so important. Alternatively, plants can be left in their pots and placed in a wide, large pot that does not have a hole in its base. This is then suspended in an attractive harness.

Both flowering and foliage trailing plants can be used; if the position is shaded, use only shade-surviving foliage plants, whereas bright and sunny places can be filled with flowering types.

Flowering houseplants for indoor hanging-baskets
- *Aeschynanthus radicans*
  Lipstick Vine
- *Aporocactus flagelliformis*
  Rat's-tail Cactus
- *Begonia tuberhybrida pendula*
  Basket Begonia
- *Campanula isophylla*
  Italian Bellflower
- *Columnea x banksii*
  Goldfish Plant
- *Columnea microphylla*
  Goldfish Plant
- *Rhipsalidopsis gaertneri*
  Easter Cactus
- *Schlumbergera truncata*
  Christmas Cactus

Foliage plants for indoor hanging-baskets
- *Asparagus densiflorus* 'Sprengeri'
  Emerald Fern
- *Ceropegia woodii*
  Rosary Vine
- *Chlorophytum comosum*
  Spider Plant
- *Epipremnum pinnatum*
  Devil's Ivy
- *Plectranthus oertendahlii*
  Swedish Ivy
- *Plectranthus coleoides* 'Marginatus'
  Variegated Swedish Ivy

- *Saxifraga stolonifera* 'Tricolor'
  Mother of Thousands
- *Senecio rowleyanus*
  String of Beads

PLANTING AN INDOOR HANGING-BASKET

1 Plan the positioning of individual plants before setting them in the basket. Draw a circle the size of the container on a piece of paper and arrange the plants.

2 Form a thin layer of gravel in the container's base to ensure water can run freely into the drip tray. If there are just a few large holes, place broken pieces of clay pots over them.

3 Stand the container on a bucket. Cover the base with peat-based potting compost, to which has been added a handful of charcoal. Also, clay particles help in moisture retention.

4 Remove the pots and first plant in the centre of the container, packing potting compost around and between each plant. Ensure each plant has been watered several hours earlier.

5 When planting trailing and cascading plants, slightly tilt them around the outside of the container, so that their stems are able to hang freely and therefore cascade attractively around the container's edge.

GROUPING PLANTS IN HANGING-BASKETS

Instead of removing plants from their pots and planting them in potting compost, plants can be stood in an ornamental pot (without a hole in its base) and suspended in an ornamental harness. The advantage of this method is that the display can be changed as soon as one of the plants stops flowering or becomes unsightly. Flowering houseplants with short seasons of flower can be displayed in this way, but also use a few foliage types to give the display permanency.

1 Draw a circle the same size as the bowl on a sheet of paper and place the plants on it. It is not necessary to create a congested group – a few distinctive plants can be equally attractive.

2 Select a flat-based bowl 25-30cm/ 10-12in wide and 13-15cm/5-7in deep. Form a 2.5cm/1in deep layer of pea-shingle in the base. Water the plants and allow to drain before putting them in the container.

3 Fill the container with plants from the centre to the outside. Pack moist peat between the pots – it helps to keep the compost cool and to reduce the amount of water they need.

4 Sphagnum moss placed around the edges makes the display more attractive. However, it is essential that the compost can be seen as the plants must be watered individually. Some plants will need more water than others.

Hydroculture

Also known as hydroponics and soil-less culture, hydroculture is an interesting and exciting way to grow houseplants. It involves growing plants with their roots in a nutrient solution instead of a potting compost.

It is an ideal way to grow houseplants if they are likely to be neglected for long periods. It is more expensive to grow houseplants in this way, although they do not need as much regular maintenance. As long as an occasional check is made to ensure that the water level is correct, there is no risk of giving your plant either too much or too little water. Also, plants are always given the right amount of chemicals to keep them healthy.

Suitable plants

Flowering houseplants
- *Aechmea fasciata*
  Urn Plant
- *Anthurium andreanum*
  Painter's Pallete
- *Anthurium scherzerianum*
  Flamingo Flower
- *Clivia miniata*
  Kaffir Lily
- *Euphorbia pulcherrima*
  Poinsettia
- *Haemanthus albiflos*
  Blood Lily
- *Hoya carnosa*
  Wax Plant
- *Saintpaulia ionantha*
  African Violet
- *Spathiphyllum wallisii*
  Peace Lily
- *Streptocarpus hybridus*
  Cape Primrose
- *Vriesea splendens*
  Flaming Sword

Foliage houseplants
- *Aglaonema* (several species)
  Chinese Evergreen
- *Aspidistra elatior*
  Cast Iron Plant
- *Brassaia actinophylla*
  Umbrella Tree
- *Cyperus diffusus*
  Umbrella Plant
- *Dieffenbachia* (several species)
  Dumb Cane
- *Dracaena* (several species)
- *Ficus deltoidea*
  Mistletoe Fig
- *Ficus elastica*
  Rubber Plant
- *Hedera helix* (several varieties)
  Common Ivy
- *Maranta leuconeura*
  Prayer Plant
- *Monstera deliciosa*
  Swiss Cheese Plant
- *Philodendron scandens*
  Sweetheart Plant
- *Pilea cadieri*
  Aluminium Plant
- *Pilea muscosa*
  Artillery Plant
- *Sansevieria trifasciata*
  Mother-in-Law's Tongue
- *Tradescantia fluminensis*
  Wandering Jew
- *Zebrina pendula*
  Silvery Inch Plant

CONVERTING A PLANT TO HYDROCULTURE

1 Carefully remove the soil-ball by inverting the plant and tapping the pot's edge on a firm surface, supporting the soil-ball with one hand and removing the pot with the other.

2 Immerse the soil-ball in a bowl of lukewarm, clean water and gently wash away the potting compost. Ensure that all soil is removed, even from between very small and fine roots. Wash them several times.

4 Fill the base of the container with thoroughly washed, expanded clay particles to a depth that enables roots to be evenly spread out. Hold the plant in a natural and eye-appealing angle.

5 Continue to dribble washed clay particles around the roots until slightly below the rim of the container. Coloured stones placed one-third up the glass jar create additional interest.

3 *Use sharp scissors to cut away damaged roots, as well as brown ones. Also, trim back long roots. To keep the size of foliage in balance with extent of the roots, trim back a few shoots.*

6 *Place large pebbles on top of the clay particles and pour in clean tap water at room temperature to cover the roots. Place in shade until plants are established and growing strongly.*

Bonsai

Bonsai trees are some of the most fascinating and interesting of all plants grown in containers.

The ancient art of growing dwarf trees began more than a thousand years ago when the Chinese transplanted seedlings of trees that had been growing in the wild into small pots. Many of these young trees had been growing in impoverished conditions and when potted into good soil grew strongly. The Chinese discovered that by constricting the roots in small containers, and regularly pruning the roots and shoots, the trees could be kept small. The Japanese began growing dwarfed trees, developing the art and conferring the name *Bonsai*, which means *growing a plant in a tray*.

Traditionally, bonsai specimens were trees that could only be taken indoors into a cool room with good light for a couple of days at a time, and then returned outside for several weeks to recover. However, in recent years *Indoor Bonsai* types have been introduced which are tropical or semi-tropical plants that can be kept indoors throughout the year. To distinguish these two types of bonsai, the traditional outdoor ones are often known as *Japanese Bonsai*, the indoor specimens as *Chinese Bonsai*. However, these terms in no way indicate the origination of the plants used in either type.

THE TOOLS YOU WILL NEED

In addition to the trees, shallow stoneware pots and a few pieces of equipment are needed. These include branch and root clippers, a leaf pruner and a root teaser. Bonsai wire, flint and perlite chippings are also needed, as well as a special potting compost.

Right: *Containers, compost and tools are essential parts of growing bonsai. These include scissors for trimming leaves and stems, clippers for severing branches, potting compost and additives to encourage both moisture retention and free drainage, and strong wire to reposition branches and stems. More specialized equipment includes devices that assist in bending stems.*

Above: *Outdoor bonsai benefit from a screen formed of slatted wood. This enables the free circulation of air and provides shade from strong sunlight.*

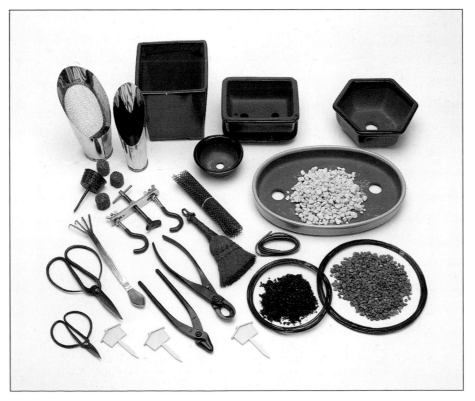

ROOT PRUNING AND REPOTTING

After its initial potting, a bonsai tree will grow in the same potting compost for several years. Thereafter, it needs repotting every two or three years, in spring or early summer when buds are swelling.

1 Water the compost a day before repotting to ensure that the potting compost is slightly moist. When added, fresh compost blends better with slightly damp compost than if dry.

6 Select a fresh pot, and if previously unused soak it in water for several days. Dry containers absorb water from the potting compost and may deprive the tree of the moisture it needs. The plant's establishment will be delayed.

2 If the tree is young and growing strongly, select a pot fractionally larger than the present one. However, with old and established trees use the same size pot, until pot bound.

3 Cut wires that negligently have been left to secure the tree, then lift out the root-ball. If necessary, run a sharp knife around the inside of the pot to sever roots adhering to it.

4 Use a root teaser – or old kitchen fork – to scrape potting compost from the roots. One-third of the roots should be exposed, both underneath as well as around the tree.

5 Use a root clipper to cut away half of the exposed roots, as well as those that are damaged. Do not unduly cut away the roots, as when repotted this may leave the tree insecure.

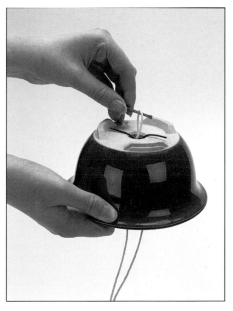

7 Cut small, square-shaped pieces of plastic-coated wire mesh, placing them over the inside of each hole. These will ensure good drainage and prevent the potting compost falling through.

8 Use small pieces of plastic-coated wire to hold these in position. From the outside of the pot's base, loop the wire through the plastic mesh, bending the ends back so that it remains secure.

9 To secure the tree firmly until its roots fill the pot, pass a piece of garden string out through the hole, around a nail, and back into the pot. Eventually, it is tied over the root-ball, firmly but not excessively tight.

*10 **Wire can also be used to secure the tree, but this must be cut away as soon as the roots are established. If left, it eventually cuts into the tree. String has the virtue of rotting.*** Continued on following page.

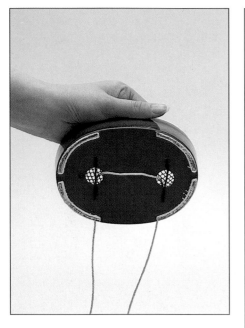

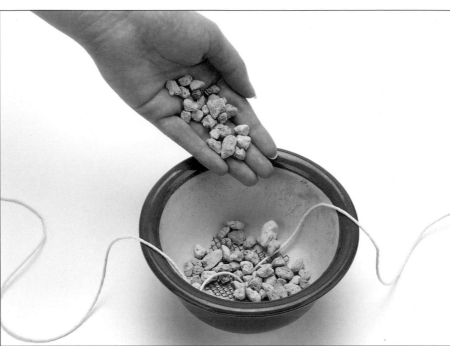

11 *Some bonsai containers have two holes in their bases. In such cases, pass the string out through one and back in the other. Ensure that the string does not bend the wire mesh.*

12 *Sprinkle a mixture of perlag or perlite and flint chippings or clean gravel in the pot's base. This* ensures good drainage and enables the limited amount of potting compost to retain moisture.

13 *Cover with a thin layer of specially prepared bonsai potting compost. There are special potting composts for deciduous, evergreen and ericaceous plants.*

15 *It is often necessary to adjust the height of the compost several times, as well as rotating the root-ball so that it is in the best position when the string is tied over it.*

16 *Pull up the two ends of the string and tie them around the root-ball. Lightly work potting compost between the roots, firming it gently. Use a small, pointed stick.*

17 *Use a sharp-ended piece of wood or special compost firmer (resembles a chopstick), to firm potting compost around roots. It is essential to remove air pockets from around roots.*

18 *Sprinkle a thin layer of 3mm/ ⅛in gravel over the surface. This helps to keep the potting compost moist during warm periods, as well as creating an attractive surface.*

14 *Adjust the level of the compost in the pot's base so that the plant's surface is slightly below the rim – about 6mm/¼in. If too high, it is difficult to water the potting compost.*

2 *Indoor bonsai in a warm room need the root-ball immersed in water at least twice a week throughout the year. It is essential that the potting compost is not allowed to become dry.*

1 *With outdoor plants, water mainly in spring and summer. In winter, water less frequently and then only in the morning. This helps to prevent the soil-ball and roots freezing. Preferably, use rainwater. However, in air-contaminated areas water often drains over dirty tiles. Therefore, it is usually better to use boiled water that has cooled to room temperature.*

19 *Initially, water the potting compost by standing the plant in a bowl shallowly filled with water. When moisture seeps to the surface, remove and allow excess to drain.*

3 *Mist spray outdoor trees only in summer and when in shade. Indoors, mist-spray throughout the year, but in winter only during mornings, so that excess moisture evaporates by evening.*

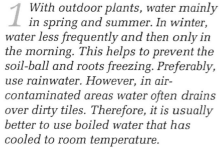
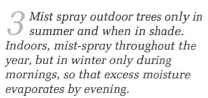

PRUNING BONSAI PLANTS

Pruning branches and shoots helps restrict a plant's size, and is necessary throughout its life. As well as creating a diminutive plant, it helps bonsai to assume a gnarled and aged appearance, part of their charm and character.

Prune flowering trees immediately the blossom fades and falls off. If these plants are pruned too early, many of the buds that later produce flowers will be cut off.

Leaf-pruning creates a 'false autumn' and encourages plants to produce a fresh set of leaves, smaller and more attractively coloured than if this job is not performed. It is carried out on deciduous trees in early or mid-summer. Remove one-third of the largest leaves, and subsequently when new leaves develop remove another one-third of these. When a further set of new leaves appears, remove the remaining large leaves. When performing this task, leave the leaf-stalks – cut off only the leaf-blades.

Evergreen plants are not leaf-pruned, nor those deciduous types grown for their fruit or flowers.

Wisterias grown as bonsai plants are very attractive, with cascades of pea-like flowers from the miniature branches. Do not allow such plants to dry out when in flower.

4 Bonsai plants benefit from a weak liquid fertilizer during spring and summer, at weekly or fortnightly intervals. Do not feed them in autumn or winter, at it encourages soft growth.

1 Branch pruning is best performed at the end of winter when the tree is starting into growth. Shorten or thin out shoots and cut out dead wood, so that the bonsai resembles a miniature tree.

WIRING PLANTS

Wiring is mainly used during a tree's formative years to alter and shape it. It involves wrapping pieces of wire around the trunk and branches to hold them in position. Deciduous trees are wired after their leaves have matured, in early summer, and removed in autumn. Evergreen types, however, take longer to assume the desired shape and are wired at the onset of winter and removed twelve or eighteen months later.

The wires are wrapped around trunks and branches in a 45 degree spiral, but care must be taken to ensure they are not too tight and cut into the bark. Conversely, if too loose they do not offer any support. Soft, tender-barked trees, such as maples, are sometimes damaged by the wires. To prevent this happening, first wrap the wires in soft tissue paper. Trunks and thick branches have thicker wire wrapped around them than have thin shoots.

OUTDOOR BONSAI PLANTS

Both evergreen and deciduous trees and shrubs are grown as bonsai subjects outdoors. Many are selected for their attractive foliage and shape, while others for their flowers or fruits. The following trees are just a few which can be grown as bonsai subjects outdoors.

• **Evergreen** trees and shrubs to choose from include Yew (*Taxus baccata*), Chinese Juniper (*Juniperus chinensis*), Japanese Cedar (*Cryptomeria japonica*), Firs (*Abies*), Spruces (*Picea*) as well as *Chamaecyparis pisifera* and *Pinus parviflora*.

• **Deciduous** trees and shrubs include the Japanese Maple (*Acer palmatum*), Beech (*Fagus sylvatica*), Elm (*Ulmus*) and Oak (*Quercus*).

• **Flowering** trees and shrubs include Winter-flowering Jasmine (*Jasminum nudiflorum*), flowering cherries and peaches.

• **Fruiting** shrubs and trees include the Herringbone Cotoneaster (*Cotoneaster horizontalis*), Firethorn (*Pyracantha*) and Crab Apple (*Malus*).

INDOOR BONSAI PLANTS

These are mainly tropical and sub-tropical plants. Like all houseplants, each desires

1 *Gently manipulate the trunk and branches into position and wrap wire around them in a spiral. If* branches are very thick, double spirals of wire are needed, spaced slightly apart.

a certain temperature range to encourage healthy growth, such as:

Up to 16°C (61°F)
Myrtus communis (Myrtle)
Nandina domestica (Sacred Bamboo/ Heavenly Bamboo)
Olea europaea (Olive)
Pistacia vera (Pistachio/Green Almond)
Podocarpus macrophyllus (Buddhist Pine/Japanese Yew)
Sageretia thea
Serissa foetida (Serissa)
Zelkova sinica (Chinese Elm)

Up to 21°C (70°F)
Carmona microphylla (Tea Tree)
Crassula arborescens (Chinese Jade/ Silver Dollar/Silver Jade)
Cycas revoluta (Sago Palm/Japanese Fern Palm)
Eugenia malaccensis (Malay Apple/ Rose Apple/Pomelac Jambos)
Ficus benjamina (Weeping Fig)
Ficus retusa (Banyan Tree/Indian Laurel/Malay Banyan)
Murraya paniculata (Orange Jasmine/ Cosmetic-bark Tree/Satinwood)
Punica granatum (Pomegranate)
Schefflera arboricola (Umbrella Tree)

Culinary herbs are mostly hardy garden plants, some becoming quite large and unsuitable for cultivating on a windowsill indoors. A few, however, are diminutive and when young can be grown indoors.

HERBS FOR THE HOME

• **Chervil** (*Anthriscus cerefolium*) is a biennial usually grown as an annual. The bright green, fern-like leaves that resemble parsley are used to flavour salads, sauces, soups and omelettes.

• **Chives** (*Allium schoenoprasum*) is a hardy perennial, with grass-like, tubular leaves having a mild onion flavour. It is added to salads as well as to cheese and egg dishes.

• **Parsley** (*Petroselinum crispum*) is really a biennial but invariably grown as an annual, with densely curled, bright green leaves which add a distinctive and spicy flavour to sauces, stuffings, savoury dishes and salads.

• **Pot Marjoram** (*Origanum onites*) is a hardy perennial with bright green leaves and white or mauve, tube-like flowers borne during midsummer. The aromatic leaves are chopped or crushed and used to flavour soups, stews, pies and stuffings.

• **Common Thyme** (*Thymus vulgaris*) is a hardy perennial with aromatic leaves used dried or fresh in stuffings for meat, as well as in casseroles. It is an important part of dried, mixed herbs.

• **Summer Savory** (*Satureja hortensis*) is a hardy annual with dark green leaves used to flavour soups, meat, fish, egg and cheese dishes, as well as for adding to stuffings.

• **Sweet Basil** (*Ocimum basilicum*) is a half-hardy annual, with shiny green, aromatic leaves used in tomato soup, omelettes, fish soups and egg dishes. In France it has been used to flavour turtle soup.

DON'T BUY PLANTS WHICH ARE ...

• unlabelled.
• pot bound, with roots coming out of drainage holes in the pot.
• weak and lanky. They probably were packed too closely together, each plant desperately trying to gain extra light by growing upwards and becoming drawn and weak.

INCREASING PARSLEY FROM SEEDS

1 Fill a pot with soil-based or peat-based seed compost. With a round soil-presser – or top of a jar – gently firm the seed compost so that its surface is 12mm/½in below the pot's rim.

3 Cover lightly with finely-sieved soil. Horticultural sieves are available, but as a substitute a kitchen type can be bought and reserved for this use – if the compost is very damp it may soon clog.

• yellowing and starved – they never recover.
• damaged by pests and diseases.
• wilting, especially if the pot is full of roots.

INCREASING INDOOR HERBS

There are several ways to increase herbs – by seeds, division and cuttings.

2 Tip a few seeds on a piece of stiff, folded paper. Tap the edge to encourage seeds to fall evenly on the surface. Do not sow near the edges, as this is where drying first occurs.

4 Water by standing the pot in a bowl shallowly filled with water. When moisture seeps to the surface, remove and allow excess to drain. Do not water seeds from above, as it will move them.

DIVIDING CHIVES

1 Chives are easily increased by dividing congested plants. Tap the pot's rim on a firm surface and remove the pot. Water the compost several hours before dividing the plant.

2 Pull the plant into several pieces, discarding old and central parts. It is better to have several well-sized pieces than to create many plants with just a few stems.

3 Fill a pot with potting compost and pot up plants individually. Repot them to the same depth as before.

Leave about 12mm/½in between the potting compost and rim. Water from above to settle the compost.

CUTTINGS OF POT MARJORAM

1 The day before taking cuttings, thoroughly water the mother plant to ensure the cuttings will not wilt. The plant must be turgid. Sever long shoots that are to be used as cuttings at the plant's base.

2 Each cutting is trimmed individually to 5-7.5cm/2-3in long. Also, remove the lower leaves, cutting them close to the stem. To avoid leaving ragged ends, always use a sharp knife.

3 Fill a pot with potting compost and firm it to within 12mm/½in of the pot's rim. Use a dibber to form holes, into which cuttings are inserted with potting compost firmed around them.

4 Water the cuttings from above, so that the potting compost settles around the base of each cutting. Allow excess water to drain and place in a warm, lightly shaded place until rooted.

Carefully looking after houseplants throughout the year only for them to die through neglect while you are holidaying away from home is a major disaster. Your plants main need while you are away on holiday is water, and although a neighbour will often act as a 'plant sitter', unless that person is experienced in looking after plants it is usually better to rig up your own watering system. Houseplant sitters who are not used to looking after indoor plants invariably excessively water them, with the result that roots rot and eventually the plants die – sometimes weeks after you return from holiday.

The length of the holiday, as well as whether in winter or summer, influences the treatment given to the plants.

Here are a few suggestions and ideas to ensure that your plants survive when you are away from home for several days or even a few weeks.

BEFORE LEAVING HOME ...

- ask a friend to turn symmetrically-shaped foliage plants a quarter of a turn every few days to prevent them becoming lop-sided.
- close the door of the room in which the plants are left, to prevent draughts drying them, as well as pets knocking them over or eating them.
- a week before leaving home, check that plants are not infested with pests or diseases. If found, spray plants immediately. Before long holidays, it is a wise precautionary measure to spray all plants, as some pests may be at their egg stage. If left unsprayed, such plants will be smothered with adult insects by your return.
- place large plants on a sheet of plastic in the centre of a room, away from south-facing windows. Place each pot in a saucer filled with water.
- small plants can be kept moist and cool for short periods by placing them in plastic seedtrays and packing moist peat around them.
- draw curtains, especially those on south-facing windows, during summer.

HOLIDAY CARE

1 Remove all faded flowers, as well as those which will be past their best by the time you expect to return. If left, they decay and encourage the rest of the plant to deteriorate, especially if it has soft leaves.*

2 Remove dead leaves from foliage plants. Those with masses of foliage are soon damaged by decaying leaves that are left in position, the rot quickly spreading.

3 Place small plants on a capillary mat, one end spread over a draining-board and the other trailing into a sink full of water, which acts as a large reservoir – ideal for long holidays.*

4 Use wicks to water plants individually. Push one end of a wick into the potting compost, the other deeply into a reservoir of water positioned higher than the plants.

5 As well as placing plants in bowls of clean water, they can also be stood on moist pebbles of expanded clay particles in shallow dishes. Both of these methods also increases the humidity.

Avoid placing the containers in draughts, as this encourages plants rapidly to use up the reserve of water.

PROBLEMS WITH PESTS & DISEASES

Prevention is much easier than trying to eliminate an established colony of pests or a severe infection from a disease. It is far better to take a few preventative measures, such as:
- buy plants only from reliable and reputable sources.
- inspect all new plants as soon as you get them home. If contaminated, isolate and treat them immediately.
- check plants regularly – perhaps when watering them – to ensure they are clean.
- don't use garden soil instead of properly prepared potting compost. Ordinary soil may be infested with pests, as well as harbouring disease spores.
- don't use infected plants as propagation material.
- don't leave dead flowers and leaves on plants – they encourage the presence of diseases.
- active pests, such as aphids, whitefly, thrips and red spider mites, soon pass from one plant to another.
- slow-moving pests often hide under leaves or in leaf-joints, as well as under pots.
- pests of potting composts are difficult to detect, their presence often only becoming apparent after damage has been done. Always check root-balls for pests when plants are being repotted.

SAFETY-FIRST WITH CHEMICALS

Always ...
- follow the manufacturer's instruction. Using chemicals at higher than recommended concentrations seldom improves the spray's effectiveness. It may even damage some plants.
- check that the chemical will not damage susceptible plants, such as succulents, palms and ferns.
- don't mix two different chemicals, unless recommended.
- keep all chemicals away from children and pets. And do not transfer chemicals into bottles children might believe to hold a refreshing drink.
- indoors, use only chemicals recommended for houseplants.
- remove all food and fruit from where the sprays are used. And do not spray wallpaper or fabrics.
- don't assume that pest-killing insecticides developed from natural plant extracts are not dangerous.
- wash out all containers, pipes and sprayers with soapy water after use. And don't use the same equipment to spray insecticides and weedkillers.
- don't spray plants when in strong sunlight.
- don't allow pets to lick or chew plants that have been newly sprayed. Many chemicals have a residual effect lasting for several weeks.
- don't spray plants if pets are in the room. Take the plant outside to treat it. Caged birds, as well as fish in tanks, are very susceptible to chemical sprays.

APPLYING INSECTICIDES

There are several ways in which to apply insecticides: by spraying, dusting, and insecticidal sticks that are pushed into the potting compost.

Insecticidal sticks are a preventative measure, while spraying and dusting are better if the plant is totally infested. Several sprays and dustings are usually needed to kill all the insects.

Aphids

Also known as greenfly, blackfly, aphis and aphides, these insect are the main pests of plants.

Description: Small, soft-bodied, sap-sucking insects, usually green but may be grey, orange or black. In homes, greenhouses and conservatories the green form is normally seen.

Damage: Soft parts such as petals, shoot tips and young leaves are mostly attacked, aphids piercing the tissue, sucking sap and causing mottling and distortion. Aphids excrete a sticky substance known

Above: *Gently push an insecticidal stick into the compost, a little way in from the edge of the pot. Take care not to damage the roots.*

Above: *Lightly dust the leaves with the insecticide. Avoid creating large blobs of dust on one leaf, while others are devoid of the insecticide.*

Above: *Place the plant in a large plastic bag before spraying it. Do not spray flowering plants, as the blooms may then be damaged.*

as honeydew, which as well as being unsightly encourages the presence of the fungal disease sooty mould (see pp. 88 and 89).

Control: Spray plants as soon as these pests are seen, using insecticides containing dimethoate, malathion, pirimiphos-methyl with pyrethrins, or resmethrin and pyrethrum. Repeat spray every 10-14 days.

Cyclamen mites

These pernicious pests attack a wide range of houseplants, including cyclamen, pelargoniums, African Violets and Busy Lizzies.

Description: Minute, eight-legged, spider-like creatures which cluster on the undersides of leaves and look like a coating of dust. Young mites are almost transparent; adult females vary from milky white to brown.

Damage: Leaves curl from the outside and become wrinkled into depressions and pockets. Infested foliage becomes darker than normal and the flowering period is shortened. The formation of flower buds is often prevented, and those that do develop are distorted and fall off.

Control: Remove and burn seriously infested leaves and flowers. Check corms kept from the previous year. Spray with malathion or insecticidal soap.

Red spider mites

Also known as greenhouse red spider mites and glasshouse red spider mites, they attack carnations, chrysanthemums and other ornamental plants, as well as tomatoes and cucumbers in greenhouses.

Description: About the size of a pinhead, they vary in colour from a transparent yellow-white through green to orange and brick-red. In winter the colour tends to be red, whereas in summer when females are breeding they are lighter in colour.

Damage: Both adult and immature mites pierce and suck the undersides of leaves, causing a fine, light mottling on upper surfaces which, if the attack is severe, become yellow and blotched. They often create webs.

Control: Daily mist-spraying plants prevents an attack developing into

epidemic proportions – but do not syringe flowers or soft and hairy leaves. Spray with derris or insecticidal soap as soon as the spiders or their damage is seen. Remove and burn seriously infected plants.

Mealy bugs

Mainly sub-tropical and tropical pests. Plants attacked include palms, ferns, vines, azaleas and hippeastrums.

Description: White, waxy, woodlice-like creatures that live in groups. If ignored they form large colonies.

Damage: Suck sap, causing distortion, loss of vigour and yellowing of the leaves. Like aphids they excrete honeydew, encouraging the presence of sooty mould (see pp. 88 and 89). They form colonies in leaf-joints, along stems and on leaves.

Control: Light infestations can be wiped off with cotton-buds or cotton-swabs dipped in methylated spirits – sometimes known as rubbing alcohol. Spray established colonies with malathion. Burn seriously infested plants.

Root mealy bugs

These are closely related to mealy bugs, but instead of attacking leaves, stems and shoots, infest roots. They mainly live on the outer roots of plants in pots, especially infesting cacti and other succulents.

Description: Resemble waxy-woodlice.

Damage: Chew roots, especially small ones. Normal root functions are upset, resulting in foliage discoloration and plants wilting. If untreated, death results.

Control: Inspect roots when plants are repotted. If a plant wilts or becomes discoloured for no apparent reason, remove the pot and check the roots. Use a solution of malathion to drench the roots and soil-ball. Repeat the treatment several times, at 10-14 day intervals.

Scale insects

The range of scale insects is wide, and plants attacked include fruit bushes and trees, ornamental trees, conifers, shrubs and roses, as well as orchids, ferns and other ornamental houseplants, indoors as well as in greenhouses, sunrooms and conservatories.

Description: First sign of attack is when

plants become sticky. Swollen, protective, waxy-brown discs can be seen, and it is under these that female scale insects produce their young.

Damage: Suck sap and produce honeydew that encourages the presence of sooty mould. Severe infestations cause speckling and yellowing of the leaves.

Control: Young scale insects at the 'crawler' stage are easiest to kill. They can be wiped away with a cotton bud dipped in methylated spirits or rubbing alcohol. Malathion also kills 'crawlers', but eradicating established colonies is difficult and plants are best burned.

Whitefly

Especially a nuisance in greenhouses, sunrooms and conservatories, infesting a wide range of plants. Tomatoes and cucumbers in greenhouses are often attacked.

Description: Moth-like, 3-6mm/⅛-¼in long, insects with wings and a white, mealy covering. When disturbed, they flutter about the host plant. Mostly found on the undersides of leaves.

Damage: Young green nymphs suck sap and excrete honeydew, encouraging the presence of sooty mould. Leaves turn yellow and fall off, as well as becoming black and messy through sooty mould.

Control: Eradication is not easy, and several sprayings at 3-5 day intervals are necessary. Spray with malathion or pyrethrum.

Thrips

Several types infest plants in conservatories, sunrooms and greenhouses, although they are not major pests indoors.

Description: Tiny, dark brown, fly-like creatures, about 3mm/⅛in long, with light coloured wings and legs. Often seen jumping or flying from plant to plant.

Damage: Thrips feed by piercing and sucking leaves and flowers, causing silvery mottling and streaking. In severe infestations, flowers are distorted. Undersides of leaves develop small globules of a red liquid that eventually turns black, creating an unsightly mess.

Control: Spray with malathion or derris, repeating several times. Infested plants with dry compost suffer most.

Vine weevils
Serious pest in both its beetle-like adult form and when young as a larvae.

Description: Adult weevils are similar to beetles, but have a short snout. Each weevil is 8-12mm/$\frac{1}{3}$-$\frac{1}{2}$in long, black and covered with short hairs that create a matt, dull appearance. Larvae are fat, legless and creamy-white, the head is brown with mouth parts adapted for chewing roots. Invariably, the larvae are seen in a semi-curled manner.

Damage: Roots, tubers, bulbs and rhizomes are seriously damaged by larvae, causing wilting and, eventually, death. Adult weevils chew flowers, stems and leaves.

Control: Immediately the larvae or adults are seen, water the compost with malathion or a soil-pest killer. Also, spray the leaves.

Earwigs
Few people have not seen an earwig. They attack outdoor plants as well as those in greenhouses, sunrooms and conservatories.

Description: Familiar pests.

Damage: Feed at night, chewing and tearing leaves and flowers.

Control: Spray with malathion, although it is often easier to pick them off. Shaking flowers and leaves in the morning soon dislodges them.

Slugs and snails
Not usually pests of houseplants, but those stood outside on patios in summer may harbour them when taken back indoors. Plants in conservatories, sunrooms and greenhouses may also become infested.

Description: Familiar pests.

Damage: They crawl and leave trails of slime, chew flowers, stems, shoots and leaves, as well as roots, tubers, bulbs and corms. They feed mainly at night, hiding under pots, boxes and plant debris during the day.

Control: Pick off and destroy. Alternatively, in greenhouses place small heaps of slug and snail bait around affected plants. Hide these under tins or slates to prevent cats and dogs eating them.

Above: *Greenfly are the most common pest of plants and can make them unsightly.*

Houseplant Diseases

Sooty mould

Black, soot-like mould that lives on honeydew excreted by aphids and other sap-sucking insects.

Damage: Leaves, stems and flowers become covered with honeydew, then sooty mould. At first, the black, sooty deposit appears in clusters, but soon spreads and merges until the whole surface is covered.

Control: Spray aphids and other sap-sucking insects. Wipe away light infestations with a damp cloth.

Rusts

Complicated diseases, seldom infesting plants indoors but frequently seen on carnations and chrysanthemums in conservatories, sunrooms and greenhouses.

Damage: Raised rings of brown or black spores. Rust permeates the tissue, reducing a plant's vigour.

Control: Remove and burn infected leaves. Increase ventilation – high humidity in sunrooms, conservatories and greenhouses encourages it. Also, do not propagate from infected plants.

Viruses

Microscopic particles that invade plants and animals, causing disorder in the tissue but seldom killing their host.

Damage: Only the results can be seen, varying from deformed growth, mottled and streaked leaves to colour changes in flowers.

Control: No treatment for virus-infected plants. Remove and burn. Spray against sap-sucking insects, such as aphids. Buy only plants that are clean and healthy, and do not propagate from infected plants.

Botrytis

Also known as Grey Mould, this fungal disease is widespread and likely to occur

Above: *Pelargonium leaf curl virus*

Below: *Rust on a chrysanthemum leaf*

Above: *Botrytis on a cyclamen*

on many plants. Spores are present in the air and, if they land on wounds or decaying tissue, enter plants.

Damage: Grey, furry mould on soft parts, especially flowers, young leaves and shoots.

Control: Cut off and destroy infected plants. Remove dead flowers – if left they encourage the presence of botrytis. Damp, still air, as well as excessive watering, also encourages it. Spray infected plants with a fungicide.

Black leg

A disease mainly of cuttings – especially pelargoniums.

Damage: Bases of stems become soft and black.

Control: Cold, wet, compacted and air-less compost creates conditions suitable for infection. Also, infected plants and unsterilized potting soil are a source of infection.

Remove and destroy seriously infected cuttings. Slightly infected tissue can be cut away from valuable cuttings. Re-insert in clean potting soil. Ensure a good circulation of air over the cuttings and keep the potting compost barely moist.

Damping off

Attacks seedlings soon after germination. May also attack established plants in greenhouses, sunrooms and conservatories.

Damage: Seedlings – especially those sown too thickly – turn black and collapse.

Control: Sow seedlings thinly in well-drained potting compost. Place in a well-ventilated position and ensure the potting compost is not excessively wet. At the first sign of damping off, remove infected seedlings, lower the temperature and improve the circulation of air.

Powdery mildew

Fungal disease producing a white, powdery coating over leaves – often on both sides.

Damage: White spores are unsightly and soon disfigure plants. Appears in spring and summer. Infects leaves, flowers and stems.

Control: Remove badly infected leaves, stems and flowers. Increase ventilation and keep the atmosphere drier.

Above: *Black leg on a young Pelargonium*

Below: *Botrytis – (Grey Mould)*

Above: *Powdery mildew on a begonia*

As well as being harmed by pests and diseases, plants also become damaged and unhealthy because they are not grown properly.

Wilting

Growing houseplants in pots throughout the year and maintaining the right degree of moisture in the potting compost is not easy. Occasionally, plants wilt through being given either too much or too little water.

A houseplant's need for water varies throughout the year. Also, the size of the plant, the size of the pot and the amount of potting compost it holds influences the frequency and amount of water needed to maintain healthy growth.

Too little water: This is the main cause of wilting. Leaves and flowers wilt, eventually reaching a point when, no matter how much water is given, the plant will not recover. Leaves become crisp and brittle.

Too much water: This is just as likely to cause wilting as too little moisture, especially in winter when plants may not be fully active and an excess of water is not quickly used.

If plants are not badly affected, withhold water until the potting compost becomes dry. Totally saturated compost can be encouraged to release moisture by removing the pot and either allowing air to circulate around the root-ball or wrapping it in absorbent paper (see pp. 20-21). Too much water encourages the onset of decay, leaves becoming soft rather than brittle.

Other causes of wilting: During very warm summer days – usually in late afternoons – houseplants with large amounts of foliage and growing in small pots may wilt slightly even though the compost is moist. This is because the plant is unable to absorb sufficient moisture to replace that lost by evaporation through the leaves. If the plant recovers by late evening or early morning, do not worry about the wilting.

Some soil pests, such as root mealy bugs, graze on roots and make plants wilt. Remove the pot and check the soil-ball. If pests are present thoroughly drench the compost with a proprietary insecticide.

Flower buds fall off

This may happen if plants are in a draught, a dry atmosphere, receive a sudden chill or are knocked. Should a plant be affected, pick up the flower buds and throw them away. If left they encourage the presence of diseases.

Leaves fall off

Occasionally, leaves fall off. If this happens quickly, it is probably due to the plant receiving a shock such as a sudden drop in temperature or being placed in a cold draught. Re-position the plant in an even, warm temperature away from draughts.

If leaves become yellow and slowly fall off, this is due to the plant being given too much water and the potting compost becoming waterlogged. Keeping plants in dark positions – and especially when combined with a lack of plant food such as nitrogen – also causes leaves to become yellow.

Remove fallen leaves and do not give the plant further water until the root-ball has become moderately dry.

Green shoots on variegated plants

If green shoots appear on variegated plants, it is usually because the plant is in too dark a condition. The remedy is to move the plant into a brighter position.

Occasionally, green shoots appear on a variegated plant, even when in good light. This is known as reversion and the offending shoots must be cut out out at their bases.

Damaged leaf surfaces

If leaves become crisp and brown, this is due to insufficient water. But if white or straw-coloured patches or spots appear this is usually because water has splashed on leaves while the plant is in strong sunlight, the moisture then acting as a lens and intensifying sunlight. However, damage can also occur solely through plants that are best in slight shade being placed in direct sunlight.

Plants that can be left in full sun on a south-facing windowsill in winter will soon become damaged if left in the same position in summer. Soft-leaved plants are soon damaged in this way.

Above: *Some plants that have been deprived of water develop crisp, brown* areas on their leaves, especially along the edges.

Above: *Plants bearing flowers or berries are soon damaged if deprived of water.* The leaves become dry and crisp and hang in an unsightly manner.

Above: *A lack of light soon causes leaves to become yellow, especially the lower ones that are furthest from the source of light.*

Above: *The soft leaves of the African Violet are soon damaged when water droplets fall on them and the plant is in strong light.*

Above: *Some of the leaves on this Bougainvillea have fallen off due to a* sudden drop in temperature. Reposition in a warm constant temperature.

Houseplant Guide

The range of houseplants is wide and each year new species and varieties are introduced and sold through garden-centres and nurseries. Some are grown for their attractive foliage, others for their brightly-coloured flowers, while a few have colourful berries.

They can be classified according to their nature, and the uses made of them in the home, conservatory, sunroom or greenhouse. These range from trailers and climbers to large, dominant and upright plants that create a focal point in a room. Some are scented and these are always welcome indoors, as well as in greenhouses and sunrooms.

Many flowering houseplants have a trailing and cascading nature that enables them to be grown in indoor hanging-baskets, in pots placed in wall-brackets, or positioned at the edges of shelves. Ensure that the plants are placed where they can be regularly watered and are not continually knocked by people walking near them.

EASY TO GROW

- ***Aporocactus flagelliformis***
(syn. *Cereus flagelliformis*)
Rat's Tail Cactus/Rattail Cactus
Funnel-shaped, 7.5cm/3in long, magenta flowers in mid and late spring
Propagation: Cuttings (pp. 56/57) and Seeds (pp. 30/31).

- ***Campanula isophylla***
Falling Stars/Italian Bellflower/Star of Bethlehem
Star-shaped, 2.5cm/1in wide, blue flowers in mid and late summer. 'Alba' has white flowers.
Propagation: Seeds (pp. 30/31) and Cuttings (pp. 42/43).

- ***Schizocentron elegans***
(syn. *Heterocentron elegans*)
Spanish Shawl
Saucer-shaped, 2.5cm/1in wide, rose-purple flowers in summer.
Propagation: Cuttings (pp. 42/43).

PLANTS NEEDING CARE

- ***Begonia limmingheana***
(syn. *Begonia glaucophylla*)
Shrimp Begonia
Clusters of 2.5cm/1in wide, coral-red flowers in winter. Glossy leaves up to 13cm/5in long.
Propagation: Cuttings (pp. 42/43).

- ***Begonia tuberhybrida pendula***
Basket Begonia
Pendent, 5-7.5cm/2-3in wide flowers in a range of colours from early to late summer.
Propagation: Cuttings (pp. 42/43) and Division of tubers.

- ***Pelargonium peltatum***
Hanging Geranium/Ivy Geranium/Ivy-leaved Geranium
Star-shaped, 2.5cm/1in wide, flowers in a wide colour range from late spring to early autumn.
Propagation: Cuttings (pp. 42/43).

Begonia limmingheana – Shrimp Begonia

- ***Rhipsalidopsis gaertneri***
(syn. *Schlumbergera gaertneri*)
Easter Cactus
Bell-shaped, 36mm/1½in wide, bright red flowers during early and mid spring. Each flower has sharply-pointed petals.
Propagation: Cuttings (pp. 56/57).

- ***Saintpaulia grotei***
Trailing African Violet
Five-petalled, violet-like flowers, 2.5cm/1in wide, in several colours from early to late summer.
Propagation: Leaf-petiole cuttings (pp. 46/47).

- ***Schlumbergera* 'Buckleyi'**
(syn. *S. hybrida*)
Christmas Cactus
Narrowly trumpet-shaped, 5-7.5cm/2-3in long, magenta or rose-coloured flowers from early winter to late winter.
Propagation: Cuttings (pp. 56/57).

- ***Schlumbergera truncata***
(syn. *Zygocactus truncatus*)
Claw Cactus/Crab Cactus/Linkleaf/Thanksgiving Cactus/Yoke Cactus.
Narrowly trumpet-shaped, 5-7.5cm/2-3in long, pink to deep red flowers, from late autumn to mid winter. The flat and jointed leaves have deeply incised edges.
Propagation: Cuttings (pp. 56/57).

PLANTS WITH A CHALLENGE

- ***Aeschynanthus radicans***
(syn. *Aeschynanthus pulcher/Trichosporum lobbianum*)
Lipstick Vine
Tubular and hooded, 36mm/1½in long, crimson flowers during late spring and early summer.
Propagation: Cuttings (pp. 42/43) and Layering (pp. 36/37).

- ***Aeschynanthus speciosus***
(syn. *Trichosporum speciosum*)
Lipstick Vine
Tubular and lipped, 5-6.5cm/2-2½in long, bright orange flowers from mid to late summer.

Columnea x banksii 'Stavanger'

Hoya bella – Miniature Wax Plant

Propagation: Cuttings (pp. 42/43) and Layering (pp. 36/37).
• ***Columnea x banksii***
Goldfish Plant
Hooded, 6.5-7.5cm/2½-3in long, orange-red flowers from late autumn to mid spring.
Propagation: Cuttings (pp. 42/43).
• ***Columnea gloriosa***
Goldfish Plant
Hooded, 5-6.5cm/2-2½in long, bright scarlet flowers from early autumn to mid spring.
Propagation: Cuttings (pp. 42/43).
• ***Columnea microphylla***
Goldfish Plant
Hooded, 3.6-5cm/1½-2in long, bright orange-scarlet flowers from late autumn to mid spring.
Propagation: Cuttings (pp. 42/43).
• ***Episcia cupreata***

Flame Violet
Tubular, 18mm/¾in wide, orange-red flowers with yellow eyes, amidst 5-10cm/2-4in long, coppery leaves with silver veins and covered with white hairs.
Propagation: Layering (pp. 36/37).
• ***Episcia dianthiflora***
(syn. *Alsobia dianthiflora*)
Lace Flower/Lace Flower Vine
Tubular, 36mm/1½in wide, white flowers with feathered edges during summer.
Propagation: Layering (pp. 36/37).
• ***Hoya bella***
Miniature Wax Flower
Star-shaped, sweetly-scented white flowers with purple or rose-crimson centres and borne in 5cm/2in wide clusters, late spring to late summer.
Propagation: Cuttings (pp. 42/43).

Columnea gloriosa – Goldfish Plant

Flowering Climbers

Twining stems, richly embroidered with colourful flowers, bring interest to rooms as well as greenhouses and conservatories. Some are vigorous and need the roof of a greenhouse or conservatory to reveal their full beauty, while others happily grow in small pots indoors.

EASY TO GROW
• *Achimenes hybrida*
Cupid's Bower/Hot Water Plant/
Monkey-faced Pansy/Widow's Tears/
Mother's Tears
Trumpet-like, about 36mm/1½in wide, in many colours from early summer to early autumn.
Propagation: Cuttings (pp. 42/43), Seeds (pp. 30/31) and Division of tubers in spring.
• *Thunbergia alata*
Black-eyed Susan
Tubular, 5cm/2in wide, orange-yellow flowers with dark centres, from early to late summer.
Propagation: Seeds (pp. 30/31).

PLANTS NEEDING CARE
• *Allamanda cathartica* 'Grandiflora'
Common Allamanda/Golden Trumpet
Trumpet-shaped and tubular, 7.5cm/3in wide, bright yellow flowers from mid to late summer.
Propagation: Cuttings (pp. 42/43).
• *Bougainvillea* 'Mrs. Butt'
Paper Flower
Papery, 2.5cm/1in wide, rose-crimson flowers in late summer and early autumn.
Propagation: Cuttings (pp. 42/43).
• *Bougainvillea glabra*
Paper Flower
Papery, 2.5cm/1in wide, flowers in shades of purple and red in late summer and early autumn.
Propagation: Cuttings (pp. 42/43).
• *Clerodendrum thomsoniae*
Bag Flower/Bleeding Heart/Glory Flower/Tropical Bleeding Heart
Lantern-like, 2.5cm/1in long, white flowers with red tips, from early to late summer.
Propagation: Cuttings (pp. 42/43).

Allamanda cathartica – Golden Trumpet

Achimenes grandiflora – Hot Water Plant

Bougainvillea 'Mrs Butt' – Paper Flower

- ***Gloriosa rothschildiana***
Climbing Lily/Flame Lily/Gloriosa Lily/Glory Lily
Turk's-cap-like, 10cm/4in long, red and yellow flowers during early and mid summer.
Propagation: Seeds (pp. 30/31) and Division of tubers in early spring.
- ***Gloriosa superba***
Climbing Lily/Flame Lily/Gloriosa Lily/Glory Lily
Turk's-cap-like, 10cm/4in long, orange and red flowers during early and mid summer.
Propagation: Seeds (pp. 30/31) and Division of tubers in early spring.

Jasminum mesnyi – Japanese Jasmine

- ***Jasminum mesnyi***
(syn. *Jasminum primulinum*)
Japanese Jasmine/Primrose Jasmine/Yellow Jasmine
Semi-double, 5cm/2in wide, yellow flowers from early to late spring.
Propagation: Cuttings (pp. 42/43).
- ***Jasminum polyanthum***
Pink Jasmine
Star-shaped, 2.5cm/1in wide, white and pale pink flowers from early autumn to late spring.
Propagation: Cuttings (pp. 42/43).
- ***Passiflora caerulea***
Blue Passion Flower/Common Passion Flower

Stephanotis floribunda – Madagascar Jasmine

Highly ornate and intricate, 7.5cm/3in wide, white and bluish-purple flowers from mid to late summer.
Propagation: Cuttings (pp. 44/45).
- ***Plumbago auriculata***
(syn. *Plumbago capensis*)
Cape Leadwort
Star-faced and tubular, 2.5cm/1in wide, pale blue flowers from early summer to autumn.
Propagation: Cuttings (pp. 42/43).

PLANTS WITH A CHALLENGE
- ***Dipladenia sanderi* 'Rosea'**
(syn. *Mandevilla sanderi* 'Rosea')
Pink Allamanda

Trumpet-shaped, 7.5cm/3in wide, pink flowers with yellow throats, from early to late summer.
Propagation: Cuttings (pp. 42/43).
- ***Hoya carnosa***
Honey Plant/Wax Plant
Star-shaped, white to flesh-pink flowers borne in upturned umbrellas from late spring to late summer.
Propagation: Cuttings (pp. 42/43).
- ***Stephanotis floribunda***
Floradora/Madagascar Jasmine/Wax Flower
Tubular, 36mm/1½in long, white flowers from late spring to early autumn.
Propagation: Cuttings (pp. 44/45).

Many climbing houseplants are densely covered with attractive leaves that form eye-catching screens to cloak unappealing features. When plants are young, canes often create enough support, but with added growth and after a few years many are best moved to a greenhouse or conservatory and given a permanent framework of wires.

EASY TO GROW

• **Cissus antarctica**
Kangaroo Vine
Green, glossy, 10cm/4in long leaves with sharply-toothed edges.
Propagation: Cuttings (pp. 44/45).

• **Cissus rhombifolia**
(syn. *Rhoicissus rhomboidea*)
Grape Ivy/Venezuela Treebine
Dark green leaves formed of three irregularly diamond-shaped leaflets.
Propagation: Cuttings (pp. 44/45).

• **Cissus rhombifolia 'Ellen Danica'**
(syn. *Rhoicissus rhomboidea* 'Ellen Danica')
Mermaid Vine
Leaflets with deeply-indentated leaflets.
Propagation: Cuttings (pp. 44/45).

• **X Fatshedera lizei**
Fat-headed Lizzie/Ivy-tree/Miracle Plant
Deep, shiny green, five-lobed leaves up to 18cm/7in long.
Propagation: Cuttings (pp. 42/43).

• **Hedera canariensis 'Variegata'**
(syn. *Hedera canariensis* 'Gloire de Marengo')
Algerian Ivy/Canary Island Ivy/Madeira Ivy
Large leaves with dark green centres, merging to silvery-grey and with white borders.
Propagation: Cuttings (pp. 42/43 and 44/45) and Layering (pp. 36/37).

• **Hedera helix**
Common Ivy/English Ivy
Many attractively variegated varieties, all with small leaves.
Propagation: Cuttings (pp. 42/43 and 44/45) and Layering (pp. 36/37).

• **Philodendron scandens**
Heartleaf Philodendron/Sweetheart Plant
Shiny-green, heart-shaped leaves, 7.5-

Philodendron scandens – Sweetheart Plant

Cissus rhombifolia – Grape Ivy

10cm/3-4in long leaves.
Propagation: Cuttings (pp. 42/53) and Layering (pp. 36/37).
• *Senecio macroglossus* **'Variegatus'**
Cape Ivy/Natal Ivy/Wax Vine
Slightly succulent, triangular, green and yellow variegated leaves.
Propagation: Cuttings (pp. 44/45).
• *Senecio mikanioides*
German Ivy/Parlor Ivy/Water Ivy
Slightly succulent green leaves with sharply-pointed lobes.
Propagation: Cuttings (pp. 44/45).

PLANTS NEEDING CARE
• *Cissus discolor*
Begonia Vine/Climbing Begonia
Spear-shaped to slightly triangular, 10-13cm/4-5in long, vivid-green leaves

X Fatshedera lizei – Ivy Tree

Epipremnum pinnatum 'Aureum'

marbled purple and white.
Propagation: Cuttings (pp. 44/45).
• *Epipremnum pinnatum* **'Aureum'**
(syn. *Epipremnum aureum/Pothos aureus/Rhaphidophora aurea/ Scindapsus aureus*)
Devil's Ivy/Golden Pothos/Pothos Vine/Taro Vine
Heart-shaped, 10-13cm/4-5in long, green leaves with yellow blotches. There are several variegated varieties.
Propagation: Cuttings (pp. 42/43).
• *Monstera deliciosa*
(syn. *Philodendron pertusum*)
Fruit Salad Plant/Hurrican Plant/Split-leaf Philodendron/Swiss Cheese Plant
Shiny green, up to 45cm/18in wide, leaves with deep indentations along the sides of mature leaves.
Propagation: Cuttings (pp. 42/43).
• *Philodendron domesticum*
(syn. *Philodendron hastatum*)
Elephant's Ear Philodendron/Spade-leaf Philodendron
Glossy green, somewhat spear-shaped leaves up to 18cm/7in long.
Propagation: Cuttings (pp. 42/43).
• *Philodendron erubescens*
Blushing Philodendron/Red-leaf Philodendron

Arrow-shaped, dark green leaves with a coppery sheen, up to 23cm/9in long.
Propagation: Cuttings (pp. 42/43).
• *Piper crocatum*
Ornamental Pepper
Slightly heart-shaped green leaves with pucked surfaces, 7.5-13cm/3-5in long.
Propagation: Cuttings (pp. 42/43 and 44/45).
• *Syngonium podophyllum*
African Evergreen/Arrowhead Vine/ Goosefoot Vine/Nephthytis
Spear-shaped shiny green leaves, later developing ear-like lobes at the stalk end. Several variegated varieties.
Propagation: Cuttings (pp. 42/43 and 44/45).

PLANTS WITH A CHALLENGE
• *Philodendron melanochrysum*
(syn. *Philodendron andreanum*)
Black Gold Philodendron
Arrow-shaped leaves, although it is mainly seen in its juvenile-leaved form with heart-shaped, velvety, dark green leaves up to 15cm/6in long. Adult leaves, up to 60cm/2ft long, green, with a coppery sheen and distinctive ivory-white veins.
Propagation: Cuttings (pp. 42/43).

These are attractive throughout the year. Many are superb for creating permanent and attractive features in sunrooms and conservatories, while others are ideal in rooms, perhaps trailing from indoor hanging-baskets, in pots positioned in wall-brackets or at the edges of shelves.

EASY TO GROW

• **Asparagus densiflorus 'Meyeri'**
(syn. *Asparagus meyeri*)
Foxtail Fern/Plume Asparagus
Bright green, needle-like leaves clustered around plume-like stems up to 45cm/1½ft long.
Propagation: Seeds (pp. 30/31) and Division (pp. 34/35).

• **Asparagus densiflorus 'Sprengeri'**
(syn. *Asparagus sprengeri*)
Asparagus Fern/Emerald Feather/ Emerald Fern
Wiry, trailing stems with bright green, needle-like leaves clustered around them.
Propagation: Seeds (pp. 30/31) and Division (pp. 34/35).

• **Callisia elegans**
Striped Inch Plant
Spear-shaped, stem-clasping leaves, 2.5-3.6cm/1-1½in long, dull green and striped white on their uppersides. Deep purple below.
Propagation: Cuttings (pp. 42/43).

• **Chlorophytum comosum**
Ribbon Plant/Spider Ivy/Spider Plant/ Walking Anthericum
Long, narrow leaves, often 30cm/12in or more long, with white and green stripes.
Propagation: Plantlets (pp. 40/41) and Division (pp. 34/35).

• **Ficus pumila**
Climbing Fig/Creeping Fig/Creeping Rubber Plant
Heart-shaped, dark green, 2.5cm/1in long leaves with prominent veins.
Propagation: Cuttings (pp. 42/43 and 44/45) and Layering (pp. 36/37).

• **Glechoma hederacea variegata**
Variegated Ground Ivy
Round to heart-shaped, hairy, 2.5cm/ 1in wide leaves, pale green and blotched white at their edges.
Propagation: Cuttings (pp. 42/43 and

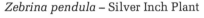
Zebrina pendula – Silver Inch Plant

44/45) and Layering (pp. 36/37).
• **Mikania ternata**
Plush Vine
Oak-shaped leaflets, 5cm/2in long, green and with a purplish sheen.
Propagation: Cuttings (pp. 42/43) and Division (pp. 34/35).

• **Nephrolepis exaltata**
Ladder Fern/Sword Fern
Sword-like, pale-green fronds up to 60cm/2ft long.
Propagation: Division (pp. 34/35).

• **Nephrolepis exaltata 'Bostoniensis'**
Boston Fern
Sword-like, arching fronds, wider than the normal species.
Propagation: Division (pp. 34/35).

• **Oplismenus hirtellus**
Basket Vine
Narrow, wavy-edged, stem-clasping leaves, about 7.5cm/3in long, with irregular white, pink and green stripes.
Propagation: Cuttings (pp. 44/45) and Division (pp. 34/35).

• **Pellaea rotundifolia**
Button Fern/New Zealand Cliff Brake

Asparagus densiflorus 'Sprengeri'

Saxifraga stolonifera 'Tricolor' – Mother of Thousands

Fern, with small, button-like, leathery, dark green fronds along wiry stems.
Propagation: Division (pp. 34/35).
- ***Philodendron scandens***
Heartleaf Philodendron/Sweetheart Plant
Shiny-green, heart-shaped, 7.5-10cm/3-4in long, leaves.
Propagation: Cuttings (pp. 42/43) and Layering (pp. 36/37).
- ***Plectranthus australis***
(syn. *Plectranthus parviflorus*)
Prostrate Coleus/Swedish Begonia/Swedish Ivy
Oval to circular, waxy, dark green leaves with light-coloured veins.
Propagation: Cuttings (pp. 42/43) and Division (pp. 34/35).
- ***Plectranthus coleoides* 'Marginatus'**
Variegated Candle Flower
Oval, hairy-surfaced light green, scallop-edged leaves with broad, white edges.
Propagation: Cuttings (pp. 42/43) and Division (pp. 34/35).
- ***Plectranthus oertendahlii***
Brazilian Coleus/Swedish Ivy
Oval to circular, scallop-edged, green leaves with prominent white veins.
Propagation: Cuttings (pp. 42/43) and Division (pp. 34/35).
- ***Saxifraga stolonifera* 'Tricolor'**
(syn. *Saxifraga sarmentosa* 'Tricolor')
Creeping Sailor/Magic Carpet/Mother of Thousands/Strawberry Begonia/Strawberry Geranium
Circular, light green leaves variegated pink and pale yellow.
Propagation: Plantlets (pp. 40/41) and Division (pp. 34/35).
- ***Setcreasea pallida* 'Purple Heart'**
Purple Heart
Lance-like and stem-clasping, rich purple leaves up to 15cm/6in long.
Propagation: Division (pp. 40/41).
- ***Soleirolia soleirolii***
(syn. *Helxine soleirolii*)
Angel's Tears/Baby's Tears/Carpet Plant/Corsican Carpet Plant/Irish Moss/Mind Your Own Business
Small, round, pale to mid-green leaves densely clustered around thin, trailing, pink stems.
Propagation: Division (pp. 34/35).
- ***Tradescantia fluminensis***
Wandering Jew

Spear-shaped, stem-clasping, 5-7.5cm/2-3in long, white-and-green striped leaves.
Propagation: Cuttings (pp. 42/43) and Division (pp. 34/35).
- ***Zebrina pendula***
Silvery Inch Plant/Wandering Jew
Spear-shaped, stem-clasping, 5cm/2in long, leaves with glistening green surfaces with silver bands.
Propagation: Cuttings (pp. 42/43) and Division (pp. 34/35).

PLANTS NEEDING CARE
- ***Ceropegia woodii***
Hearts Entangled/Hearts-on-a-string/Rosary Vine/String of Hearts
Heart-shaped, fleshy, dark green leaves, 18mm/¾in long, blotched with silver.

Chlorophytum comosum – Spider Plant

Propagation: Seeds (pp. 30/31) and Division (pp. 34/35) but avoid damaging the tubers.
- ***Epipremnum pinnatum* 'Aureum'**
(syn. *Epipremnum aureum/Pothos aureus/Rhaphidophora aurea/Scindapsus aureus*)
Devil's Ivy/Golden Pothos/Pothos Vine/Taro Vine
Heart-shaped, 10-13cm/4-5in long, green leaves with yellow blotches. There are several variegated varieties.
Propagation: Cuttings (pp. 42/43).
- ***Gynura aurantiaca***
Purple Passion Vine
Triangular, 10-13cm/4-5in long, dark green leaves smothered with purplish hairs.
Propagation: Cuttings (pp. 42-45).

- ***Gynura procumbens***
(syn. *Gynura sarmentosa*)
Velvet Plant
Triangular, 10cm/4in long, dark green leaves covered with purplish hairs.
Propagation: Cuttings (pp. 42-45).
- ***Peperomia scandens* 'Variegata'**
Cupid Peperomia
Heart-shaped, waxy-surfaced, 5cm/2in long, green leaves with yellow edges.
Propagation: Cuttings (pp. 42/43 and 44/45).
- ***Sedum morganianum***
Beaver's Tail/Burro's Tail/Donkey's Tail/Horse's Tail/Lamb's Tail
Cylindrical, fleshy, grey-green, 18mm/¾in long leaves tightly clustered around trailing stems.
Propagation: Leaf-cuttings (pp. 56/57).
- ***Sedum sieboldii mediovariegatum***
Japanese Sedum
Circular to heart-shaped, 18mm/¾in long, cream and green leaves on trailing stems.
Propagation: Leaf-cuttings (pp. 56/57).
- ***Senecio rowleyanus***
String of Beads
Grape-like, glaucous-green leaves on thread-like trailing stems.
Propagation: Trailing stems root readily.

PLANTS WITH A CHALLENGE
- ***Fittonia verschaffeltii***
Mosaic Plant/Painted Leaf/Silver Nerve/Silver Net Plant
Oval, olive-green leaves, about 5cm/2in long, with pink veins.
Propagation: Division (pp. 34/35). Trailing stems root readily.
- ***Fittonia verschaffeltii* 'Argyroneura'**
(syn. *Fittonia argyroneura*)
Nerve Plant/Silver Net Leaf
Oval, green leaves, about 5cm/2in long, with white veins.
Propagation: Division (pp. 34/35). Trailing stems root readily.
- ***Fittonia verschaffeltii* 'Argyroneura Nana'**
(syn. *Fittonia argyroneura nana*)
Snakeskin Plant
Oval, green leaves, about 2.5cm/1in long, with white veins.
Propagation: Division (pp. 34/35). Trailing stems root readily.

Architectural Plants

Large and dominant foliage plants can become permanent features indoors, often creating eye-catching focal points. Some, such as large palms, are superb when seen against a white background, while others are densely drenched in leaves and better when forming screens.

EASY TO GROW

- **Cyperus alternifolius**
Umbrella Grass/Umbrella Palm/ Umbrella Plant/ Umbrella Sedge
Narrow, grass-like bracts in umbrella-like heads.
Propagation: Seeds (pp. 30/31) and Division (pp. 34/35).

- **X Fatshedera lizei**
Fat-headed Lizzie/Ivy-tree/Miracle Plant
Deep, shiny green, five-lobed leaves up to 18cm/7in long.
Propagation: Cuttings (pp. 42/43).

- **Fatsia japonica**
False Castor Oil Plant/Formosa Rice Tree/Glossy-leaved Paper Plant/ Japanese Aralia/Japanese Fatsia/Paper Plant
Deeply-lobed, glossy-green leaves, often 30cm/12in wide on mature plants.
Propagation: Seeds (pp. 30/31) and detachment of sucker-like shoots in spring.

- **Grevillea robusta**
Silk Oak/Silky Oak
Finely dissected, mid to deep green leaves.
Propagation: Seeds (pp. 30/31).

- **Yucca aloifolia**
Dagger Plant/Spanish Bayonet
Narrow, stiff and tough leaves.
Propagation: Cane cuttings (pp. 58/59) and removal and rooting of offsets.

- **Yucca elephantipes**
Spineless Yucca
Narrow, stiff, tough, rough-edged leaves up to 90cm/3ft long.
Propagation: Cane cuttings (pp. 58/59) and removal and rooting of offsets.

PLANTS NEEDING CARE

- **Araucaria heterophylla**
(syn. *A. excelsa*)
Australian Pine/House Pine/Norfolk Island Pine
Conifer, with awl-shaped, bright green needles borne on tiered branches.
Propagation: Seeds (pp. 30/31).

- **Ardisia crenata**
(syn. *A. crispa/A. crenulata*)
Coral Berry/Spice Berry
Lance-like, stiff, wavy-edged, dark green leaves.
Propagation: Seeds (pp. 30/31).

- **Brassaia actinophylla**
(syn. *Schefflera actinophylla*)
Umbrella Plant/Umbrella Tree
Oval to oblong, glossy, mid-green leaflets. These are arranged in threes or fives at the ends of leaf-stalks.
Propagation: Seeds (pp. 30/31).

- **Dizygotheca elegantissima**
(syn. *Aralia elegantissima*)
False Aralia/Finger Aralia
Young leaves are narrow, saw-edged, coppery and delicate, but with maturity become dark green and wider.
Propagation: Seeds (pp. 30/31).

- **Ficus benjamina**
Benjamin Tree/Java Fig/Small-leaved Rubber Plant/Weeping Fig
Elliptic and pointed, 10cm/4in long, dark green leaves, soft green when young.
Propagation: Cuttings (pp. 42/43 and 44/45).

- **Ficus deltoidea**
(syn *F. diversifolia*)
Mistletoe Fig/Mistletoe Rubber Fig
Pear-shaped, leathery, dark green leaves.
Propagation: Cuttings (pp. 42/43 and 44/45).

- **Ficus elastica**
Assam Rubber/India Rubber Tree/ Rubber Plant
Oval and wide, leathery, 25-30cm/10-12in long, shiny, dark green leaves.
Propagation: Air layering (pp. 38/39).

- **Ficus lyrata**
Fiddleback Fig/Fiddleleaf Fig
Fiddle-shaped, wavy-edged, glossy, dark green leaves up to 38cm/15in long.
Propagation: Air layering (pp. 38/39)

Monstera deliciosa – Swiss Cheese Plant

Brassaia actinophylla – Umbrella Plant

Cyperus alternifolius – Umbrella Grass

Ficus elastica – Rubber Plant

and Cuttings (pp. 44/45).
- ***Howeia belmoreana***
(syn. *Howea belmoreana/Kentia belmoreana*)
Belmore Sentry Palm/Curly Palm/Sentry Palm
Narrow and pointed, dark green leaflets that create leaves 45cm/18in by 30cm/12in.
Propagation: Seeds (pp. 30/31).
- ***Howeia forsteriana***
(syn. *Howea forsteriana/Kentia forsteriana*)
Forster Sentry Palm/Kentia Palm/Paradise Palm/Thatch-leaf Palm
Narrow and pointed, dark green leaflets – wider than with *H. forsteriana*.

Similar to *Howeia belmoreana*, although the leaflets are drooping but fewer of them.
Propagation: Seeds (pp. 30/31).
- ***Monstera deliciosa***
(syn. *Philodendron pertusum*)
Fruit Salad Plant/Hurrican Plant/Split-leaf Philodendron/Swiss Cheese Plant
Shiny green, up to 45cm/18in wide, leaves with deep indentations along the sides of mature leaves. Juvenile leaves have entire edges.
Propagation: Cuttings (pp. 42/43).
- ***Phoenix canariensis***
Canary Date Palm/Canary Island Date
Straight and stiff, mid-green leaflets.
Propagation: Seeds (pp. 30/31).

- ***Schefflera arboricola***
(syn. *Heptapleurum arboricola*)
Parasol Plant
Oval to oblong, pointed, glossy-green leaflets borne in groups of nine at the ends of leaf-stalks.
Propagation: Seeds (pp. 30/31).

PLANTS WITH A CHALLENGE
- ***Dracaena deremensis***
Dragon Tree
Sword-like leaves up to 45cm/18in long, glossy green with two longitudinal silvery-white stripes.
Propagation: Cane cuttings (pp. 58/59) and removal and rooting of basal shoots in spring.

Scented Houseplants

Many indoor plants fill houses, greenhouses and conservatories with rich scents. There are scented houseplants for all seasons, many creating heady and sweet bouquets in winter when rich fragrancies are especially welcome. Some scented plants become permanant features, regularly filling a room with scent, while others are temporary and discarded after flowers fade.

There are also plants with leaves that reveal distinctive scents. Chief among these are scented-leaved pelargoniums.

EASY TO GROW

• *Exacum affine*
Arabian Violet/German Violet/Persian Violet
Saucer-shaped, purple, yellow-centred, sweetly-scented flowers from mid to late summer. The scent is like that of Lily-of-the-Valley.
Propagation: Seeds (pp. 30/31).

• *Hyacinthus orientalis*
Dutch Hyacinth/Hyacinth
Wax-like, five-petalled flowers, tightly clustered in spire-like heads, from mid winter to late spring. Sweet, heady and penetrating bouquet.
Propagation: Seeds, but only use fresh bulbs for forcing each year.

• *Pelargonium capitatum*
Rose Geranium/Rose-scented Geranium
Leaves rose-scented when bruised.
Propagation: Cuttings (pp. 42/43).

• *Pelargonium crispum*
Lemon Geranium/Lemon-scented Geranium
Leaves lemon-scented when bruised.
Propagation: Cuttings (pp. 42/43).

• *Pelargonium x fragrans*
Nutmeg Geranium
Leaves nutmeg scented when bruised.
Propagation: Cuttings (pp. 42/43).

• *Pelargonium graveolens*
Rose Geranium/Sweet-scented Geranium
Leaves rose-scented when bruised.
Propagation: Cuttings (pp. 42/43).

• *Pelargonium tomentosum*
Herb-scented Geranium/Mint Geranium/Peppermint Geranium
Leaves peppermint scented when bruised.

Propagation: Cuttings (pp. 42/43).

• *Primula x kewensis*
Primula
Yellow flowers from early winter to mid spring, with a delicate and sweet bouquet.
Propagation: Seeds (pp. 30/31).

• *Primula malacoides*
Baby Primrose/Fairy Primrose
Fragrant, star-like flowers – in a wide colour range – from early winter to midspring, with a sweet bouquet.
Propagation: Seeds (pp. 30/31).

PLANTS NEEDING CARE

• *Ardisia crenata*

Exacum affine – Persian Violet

(syn. *A. crispa/A. crenulata*)
Coral Berry/Spice Berry
Very sweet bouquet to the star-like, creamy-white flowers in early summer.
Propagation: Seeds (pp. 30/31).

• *Cyclamen persicum* (Kaori strain)
Cyclamen/Florist's Cyclamen/Persian Violet
Delicate and sweet bouquet to the winter and spring flowers.
Propagation: Seeds (pp. 30/31).

• *Freesia x hybrida*
(syn. *Freesia x kewensis*)
Freesia
Very sweet bouquet to the funnel-shaped, mid winter to mid spring,

flowers.
Propagation: Seeds (pp. 30/31) and removal of cormlets.

• *Jasminum polyanthum*
Pink Jasmine
Sweet and penetrating bouquet to the late autumn to mid spring, white and pale pink flowers.
Propagation: Cuttings (pp. 42/43).

• *Nerium oleander*
Oleander/Rosebay
Clusters of sweet, single, white flowers from early summer to autumn. Beware of the poisonous sap and wood.
Propagation: Seeds (pp. 30/31) and Cuttings (pp. 42/43).

Primula x kewensis

Jasminum polyanthum

- **Senecio rowleyanus**
String of Beads
Sweetly-scented white flowers from late summer to late autumn.
Propagation: Trailing stems readily root.

PLANTS WITH A CHALLENGE
- **Cestrum parqui**
Willow-leaved Jassamine
Greenish-yellow flowers with a sweet, night fragrance from mid to late summer.
Propagation: Cuttings (pp. 44/45).
- **Gardenia jasminoides**
Cape Jasmine/Gardenia
Heavily sweet, 7.5cm/3in wide white flowers during early and mid-summer.
Propagation: Cuttings (pp. 42/43).
- **Hoya bella**
Miniature Wax Flower
Star-shaped, sweetly-scented white flowers in 5cm/2in wide clusters from late spring to late summer.

Propagation: Cuttings (pp. 42/43).
- **Hoya carnosa**
Honey Plant/Wax Plant
Sweetly-scented, star-shaped, white to flesh-pink flowers borne in upturned umbrellas from late spring to late summer.
Propagation: Cuttings (pp. 42/43).
- **Pittosporum tobira**
Australian Laurel/House-blooming Mock Orange/Japanese Pittosporum/Mock Orange
Creamy-white flowers with an orange fragrance from mid spring to mid summer.
Propagation: Cuttings (pp. 42/43).
- **Stephanotis floribunda**
Floradora/Madagascar Jasmine/Wax Flower
Tubular, 36mm/1½in long, white flowers, with a heavily sweet fragrance, from late spring to early autumn.
Propagation: Cuttings (pp. 44/45).

Primula malacoides – Fairy Primrose

These reveal how Nature has adapted some plants to live in places where their roots are unable to absorb nutrients. Some, such as the Venus Fly Trap, use hinged jaws to capture insects, others employ sticky surfaces or pitcher-like heads that trap and prevent the escape of insects. They are not easy to grow indoors in a dry atmosphere, and need to be watered with rainwater and kept moist and humid. Take care not to expose them to aerosols.

PLANTS NEEDING CARE
• *Dionaea muscipula*
Venus Fly Trap
Hinged jaws that trap flies. Open jaws close when an insect touches trigger hairs inside them. Digestive juices break down the insect's body and the plant absorbs the nutrients. The jaws eventually re-open to trap further insects.

Propagation: Seeds (pp. 30/31) and Division (pp. 34/35).

PLANTS WITH A CHALLENGE
• *Darlingtonia californica*
(syn. *Chrysamphora californica*)
Californian Pitcher Plant/Cobra Lily/ Cobra Orchid/Hooded Pitcher Plant
It has hoods that resemble a cobra's head, heavily-veined, yellowish or pale green and up to 60cm/2ft high. There is an opening on the underside of each hood, and any insect venturing inside is doomed to become a meal for the plant. Downward-pointing hairs make it difficult for an insect to escape.

Sarracenia purpurea – Huntsman's Cup

Drosera capensis – Sundew

Propagation: Seeds (pp. 30/31) and Division (pp. 34/35).

• *Drosera binata*
(syn. *D. dichotoma/D. intermedia*)
Giant Fork-leaved Sundew
It gains it name from the way the deeply-lobed leaves divide at their tops into two or four segments. Sticky hairs on the leaves trap and digest insects. White flowers appear at the tops of long stems from early to late summer.
Propagation: Seeds (pp. 30/31) and Division (pp. 34/35).

• *Drosera cupensis*
Sundew
Rosettes of leaves covered with red, glandular hairs that both trap and disgest insects. During mid summer purple flowers are borne on stems up to 38cm/15in high.
Propagation: Seeds (pp. 30/31) and Division (pp. 34/35).

• *Sarracenia x catesbaei*
(syn. *Sarracenia hybrida*)
Pitcher Plant
A hybrid between *S. purpurea* and *S. flava*. Long, green to dark purple pitchers, with nearly erect lids, veined in purple. During spring, large yellow and purple flowers appear on long, upright and stiff stems.
Propagation: Seeds (pp. 30/31) and Division (pp. 34/35).

• *Sarracenia flava*
Huntsman's Horn/Trumpet Leaf/ Umbrella Trumpets/Watches/Yellow Pitcher Plant
Long, yellow-green or yellow pitchers, with purple or crimson veining in their throats. Each has an erect lid. Insects fall into a solution of pepsin. In mid and late spring it develops yellow, nodding flowers on long stems.
Propagation: Seeds (pp. 30/31) and Division (pp. 34/35).

• *Sarracenia purpurea*
Huntsman's-cup/Indian Cup/Pitcher Plant/Side-saddle Flower
Semi-erect, purple and green pitchers. In spring it develops greenish-purple, nodding flowers on long, erect stems. Like all pitchers plants, insects fall into a pepsin solution, drown and are digested by the plant.
Propagation: Seeds (pp. 30/31) and Division (pp. 34/35).

Sarracenia flava – Huntsman's Horn

Dionaea muscipula – Venus Fly Trap

Botanically, fruits are mature ovaries (female part of a flower). They bear ripe seeds and may be soft and fleshy or dry pods. Berries, however, are fleshy and juicy fruits.

To most houseplant enthusiasts these are synonymous and refer to any plant that reveals colourful and attractive berries. They range from bright red berries to orange-like fruits. Do not expect to grow types that can be eaten, as high humidity and temperatures are usually needed. Nevertheless, they bring an attractive and unusual feature to the home.

EASY TO GROW
• *Nertera depressa*
(syn. *Nertera granadensis/Gomozia granadensis*)
Bead Plant
Creeping evergreen with small, oval to rounded, light green leaves. Insignificant greenish-yellow flowers appear in early summer, followed by glossy, bright orange berries during

Solanum capsicastrum – Winter Cherry

autumn and well into winter.
Propagation: Division (pp. 34/35).
• *Rhipsalis cassutha*
(syn. *R. baccifera*)
A member of the *Cactaceae* family, in the wild trailing for up to 7.5m/25ft but much less when grown in a small pot indoors. Pale green, cylindrical stems bear creamy flowers in summer, followed by small, round, white fruits
Propagation: Cuttings (pp. 56/57).

PLANTS NEEDING CARE
• *Ardisia crenata*
(syn. *A. crispa/A. crenulata*)
Coral Berry/Spice Berry
Shrub-like houseplant with a very sweet bouquet to the star-like, creamy-white flowers in early summer. These are followed by long-lasting, glossy, scarlet berries that crowd on stiff stalks.
Propagation: Seeds (pp. 30/31).
• *Capsicum annuum*
Chilli/Christmas Pepper/Green Pepper/Ornamental Pepper/Red Pepper
Short-lived, shrubby perennial usually

Ardisia crenata – Coral Berry

treated as an annual and grown for its decorative, red, green or yellow fruits that appear during autumn and into winter. Fruits range in shape – spherical, conical with twisted or wrinkled surfaces.
Propagation: Seeds (pp. 30/31).
• *Ficus deltoidea*
(syn *F. diversifolia*)
Mistletoe Fig/Mistletoe Rubber Fig
Shrub-like with pear-shaped, leathery, dark green leaves. Throughout the year, yellow or dull red berry-like fruits about 12mm/½in long are borne on long stalks from the upper leaf-joints.
Propagation: Cuttings (pp. 42/43 and 44/45).

• *Solanum capsicastrum*
Winter Cherry
A half-hardy evergreen shrub that produces attractive fruits in winter. Initially, these are marble-like, slightly-pointed and green, slowly turning orange-red.
Propagation: Seeds (pp. 30/31).

PLANTS WITH A CHALLENGE
• *X Citrofortunella mitis*
(syn. *Citrus mitis*)
Calamondin Orange/Panama Orange
Widely-known citrus fruit – usually sold as *Citrus mitis* – for growing indoors,in greenhouses and

conservatories, as it flowers and bears fruits while still small. Highly-scented white flowers are borne throughout the year and followed by round, 25-36mm/1-1½in wide, fruits that slowly change from dark green to orange-yellow.
Propagation: Cuttings (pp. 42/43).
• ***Citrus limon* 'Meyeri'**
(syn. *Citrus meyeri*)
Chinese Dwarf Lemon/Dwarf Lemon/Meyer Lemon
This is a dwarf lemon, ideal as a houseplant but especially suitable for growing in greenhouses or conservatories. It has dark green leaves and highly scented, red-flushed, white flowers in spring and early summer. The fruits are dark green at first and take many months to ripen, but don't expect them to be anything but ornamental.
Propagation: Cuttings (pp. 42/43).

Ficus deltoidea – Mistletoe Fig

Nertera depressa – Bead Plant

X Citrofortunella mitis – Calamondin Orange

Capsicum annuum – Christmas Pepper

South-facing windowsills are the brightest positions in a home, but can be too bright for some plants. Houseplants suggested here happily live within 60cm/2ft of windows facing south. However, plants such as desert cacti (types that grow in semi-desert regions and at ground-level), succulent plants and pelargoniums thrive on windowsills.

IF IT'S TOO BRIGHT ...

- net curtains help to make south-facing windows suitable for a wider range of plants in summer.
- leaves become pale.
- thin leaves become shrivelled and dry, eventually falling off.
- leaves wilt, especially at midday and in afternoons.

EASY TO GROW
- **Astilbe japonica**
Spiraea
Plume-like, feathery heads of flowers in red, pink or white in late winter and early spring. Do not confuse this plant with garden shrubs in the genus *Spiraea*.
Propagation: Division (pp. 34/35).
- **Aucuba japonica 'Variegata'**
(syn. *A. japonica* 'Maculata')
Gold Dust Plant/Gold Dust Tree/ Spotted Laurel
Lance-like, shiny-green leaves with yellow spots.
Propagation: Cuttings (pp. 42/43) – with heels.
- **Cacti (Desert Types)**
There are many interestingly-shaped cacti to choose from within this group, including those in families *Chamaecereus, Echinopsis, Lobivia, Mammillaria, Notocactus, Parodia* and *Rebuntia*.
Propagation: Seeds (pp. 30/31) and Cuttings (pp. 56/57).
- **Celosia argentea cristata**
(syn. *Celosia cristata*)
Cockscomb/Woolflower
Cock's-comb-like flowers, in shades of red, orange or yellow, from mid to late summer.

Hibiscus rosa-sinensis – Chinese Rose

Propagation: Seeds (pp. 30/31).
- **Chrysanthemum**
All-year-round types in pots are available throughout the year. Wide colour range.
Propagation: Cuttings (pp. 42/43).
- **Coleus blumei**
Flame Nettle/Painted Leaves/Painted Nettle
Nettle-like leaves in a wide colour range. Plants are widely available in summer.
Propagation: Cuttings (pp. 42/43) and Seeds (pp. 30/31).
- **Daffodils**
Large, trumpet-like flowers, mainly in yellow.
Propagation: Bulbils, but use fresh bulbs each year.
- **Hippeastrum hybrida**
Amaryllis/Barbados Lily
Large, trumpet-shaped flowers at the tops of stiff stems. Some flower in summer and autumn. Wide colour range.
Propagation: Offsets, but use fresh bulbs each year.

- **Hyacinthus orientalis**
Dutch Hyacinth/Hyacinth
Erect spires of sweetly-scented flowers, mid winter to early spring.
Propagation: Plant fresh bulbs each year.
- **Impatiens walleriana**
(syn. *Impatiens holstii*)
Busy Lizzie/Busy Lizzy/Patient Lucy/ Sultana/Zanzibar Balsam
Flat-faced, trumpet-like flowers prolifically borne from mid spring to early autumn. Wide colour range.
Propagation: Seeds (pp. 30/31) and Cuttings (pp. 42/43).
- **Iresine herbstii**
Beefsteak Plant/Blood Leaf
Notch-topped, oval, wine-red leaves. *I. herbstii aureoreticulata*, the Chicken Gizzard plant, has yellowish leaves.
Propagation: Cuttings (pp. 42/43).
- **Sansevieria trifasciata**
Bowstring Hemp/Devil's Tongue/Good-luck Plant/Mother-in-Law's Tongue/ Snake Plant
Stiff, upright, broad, green stems mottled with grey, transverse bands.

'Laurentii' has creamy-white edges to the leaves.
Propagation: Cross-sections of leaves (pp. 54/55) and Division (pp. 34/35).
- **Schizanthus pinnatus**
Butterfly Flower/Poor Man's Orchid
Brightly-coloured, orchid-like flowers, marked and spotted, rose, purple and yellow, on bushy plants in spring or late summer.
Propagation: Seeds (pp. 30/31).
- **Succulents**
Many interestingly-shaped plants, in families such as *Agave, Aloe, Ceropegia, Bryophyllum, Crassula, Echevaria, Euphorbia, Gasteria, Lithops, Sempervivum* and *Sedum*.
Propagation: Seeds (pp. 30/31), Plantlets (pp. 40/41) and Cuttings (pp. 56/57).
- **Tolmiea menziesii**
Pickaback Plant/Piggyback Plant/ Thousand Mothers/Youth-on-age
Maple-like, bright green leaves. Plantlets grow on the upper surfaces, and can be removed and rooted.
Propagation: Plantlets (pp. 40/41).
- **Tulips**
Tulips such as Early Single, Early Double, Darwin and Lily-flowered types can be encouraged to flower indoors.

Fatsia japonica – False Castor Oil Plant

Propagation: Use fresh bulbs each year.

PLANTS NEEDING CARE

• *Codiaeum variegatum pictum*
Croton/Jacob's Coat/Variegated Laurel
Colourful, leathery, shiny leaves, variously shaped. Wide range of varieties.
Propagation: Cuttings (pp. 42/43).

• *Cordyline fruticosa*
(syn. *Cordyline terminalis/Draceaena terminalis*)
Good Luck Plant/Flaming Dragon Tree/Hawaiian Good Luck Plant/Ti Plant/Tree of Kings
Palm-like trunk bearing lance-shaped, mid to deep green leaves suffused with red, purple or cream. Several attractive varieties.
Propagation: Cane Cuttings (pp. 58/59) and detaching and repotting sucker-like shoots in spring.

• *Euphorbia pulcherrima*
Christmas Flower/Christmas Star/Lobster Plant/Mexican Flameleaf/Poinsettia
Brightly-colour bracts clustered at the tops of plants, mainly scarlet but also white or pink. Flowering mainly at Christmas.

Hippeastrum hybrida – Amaryllis

Propagation: Cuttings (pp. 42/43).
• *Hibiscus rosa-sinensis*
Blacking Plant/China Rose/Chinese Hibiscus/Rose of China
Large, trumpet-shaped, pink, red, white, yellow or orange flowers, often 13cm/5in wide, from early to late summer.
Propagation: Cuttings (pp. 42/43) – with heels.

• *Hypoestes phyllostachya*
(syn. *H. sanguinolenta*)
Flamingo Plant/Freckle Face/Measles Plant/Pink Dot/Polka-dot Plant
Dull green leaves irregularly peppered with pink spots.
Propagation: Cuttings (pp. 42/43).

• *Rhododendron simsii*
Azalea/Indian Azalea
Tightly packed flowers, in colours including white, orange, pink or red. Plants are encouraged to flower during winter.
Propagation: Cuttings (pp. 42/43).

• *Vallota speciosa*
(syn. *V. purpurea*)
Scarborough Lily
Cup to trumpet-shaped flowers clustered at the tops of stiff, upright

Cordyline fruticosa – Good Luck Plant

stems from mid to late summer.
Propagation: Removal of offsets when repotting.

PLANTS WITH A CHALLENGE

• *Beloperone guttata*
(syn. *Justicia brandegeana*)
False Hop/Mexican Shrimp Plant/Shrimp Plant
Distinctive, shrimp-like flowers from mid spring to late autumn.
Propagation: Cuttings (pp. 42/43).

OTHER PLANTS TO CONSIDER

EASY TO GROW
• *Aporocactus flagelliformis* (pp. 94/95)
• *Callisia elegans* (pp. 100/101)
• *Exacum affine* (pp. 104/105)
• *X Fatshedera lizei* (pp. 102/103)
• *Fatsia japonica* (pp. 102/103)
• *Grevillea robusta* (pp. 102/103)
• *Nertera depressa* (pp. 108/109)
• *Oplimenus hirtellus* (pp. 100/101)
• *Pelargonium capitatum* (pp. 104/105)
• *Pelargonium crispum* (pp. 104/105)
• *Pelargonium x fragrans* (pp. 104/105)
• *Pelargonium graveolens* (pp. 104/105)
• *Pelargonium tomentosum* (pp. 104/105)
• *Primula x kewensis* (pp. 104/105)
• *Primula malacoides* (pp. 104/105)
• *Rhipsalis cassutha* (pp. 108/109)
• *Thunbergia alata* (pp. 96/97)

Rebuntia senelis – Fire-crown Cactus

• *Tradescantia fluminensis* (pp. 100/101)
• *Setcreasea pallida* 'Purple Heart' (pp. 100/101)
• *Yucca aloifolia* (pp. 102/103)
• *Yucca elephantipes* (pp. 102/103)
• *Zebrina pendula* (pp. 100/101)

PLANTS NEEDING CARE
• *Allamanda cathartica* 'Grandifolia' (pp. 96/97)
• *Bougainvillea* 'Mrs Butt' (pp. 96/97)
• *Bougainvillea glabra* (pp. 96/97)
• *Capsicum annuum* (pp. 108/109)
• *Ceropegia woodii* (pp. 100/101)
• *Freesia x hybrida* (pp. 104/105)
• *Jasminum mesnyi* (pp. 96/97)
• *Jasminum polyanthum* (pp. 96/97 and 104/105)
• *Passiflora caerulea* (pp. 96/97)
• *Pelargonium peltatum* (pp. 94/95)
• *Plumbago auriculata* (pp. 96/97)
• *Rhipsalidopsis gaertneri* (pp. 94/95)
• *Schlumbergera* 'Buckleyi' (pp. 94/95)
• *Schlumbergera truncata* (pp. 94/95)
• *Sedum morganianum* (pp. 100/101)
• *Sedum sieboldii mediovariegatum* (pp. 100/101)
• *Senecio rowleyanus* (pp. 100/101)
• *Solanum capsicastrum* (pp. 108/109)

PLANTS WITH A CHALLENGE
• *X Citrofortunella mitis* (pp. 108/109)
• *Citrus limon* (pp. 108/109)

These positions are between 60cm/2ft and 1.2m/4ft from a bright south-facing window, or much closer to a north-facing one. The light is bright, but not created by strong and direct sun rays. Here is a range of plants that will live in these conditions.

EASY TO GROW

• **Begonia masoniana**
Iron Cross Begonia
Somewhat triangular and lop-sided, crinkly-surfaced, mid-green leaves prominently embossed with a deep purple-bronze cross.
Propagation: Whole-leaf cuttings (pp. 48/49), Leaf-squares (pp. 52/53) and Leaf-triangles (pp. 50/51).

• **Begonia rex**
King Begonia/Painted Leaf Begonia/Rex Begonia
Somewhat triangular and lop-sided leaves, usually colourfully zoned.
Propagation: Whole-leaf cuttings (pp. 48/49), Leaf-squares (pp. 52/53) and Leaf-triangles (pp. 50/51).

Plectranthus coleoides 'Marginatus'

• **Calceolaria x herbeohybrida**
(syn. *C. x hybrida*)
Pocketbook Flower/Pouch Flower/Slipper Flower/Slipperwort
Distinctive, pouch-like flowers in bright colours, such as yellow, orange, red or white, and peppered and blotched with other colours, from late spring to mid summer.
Propagation: Seeds (pp. 30/31).

• **Kalanchoe blossfeldiana**
Flaming Katy
Oval, scalloped-edged, slightly succulent dark green leaves. Tubular, scarlet flowers borne in dense heads, normally from late winter to late spring but plants can be encouraged to flower throughout the year. Varieties in pink, white or yellow.
Propagation: Seeds (pp. 30/31).

• **Pilea microphylla**
(syn. *P. muscosa*)
Artillery Plant/Gunpowder Plant
Fern-like, bushy plant with yellow-green flowers from late spring to late summer.

Propagation: Cuttings (pp. 42/43).

• **Senecio cruentus**
(syn. *Cineraria cruenta*)
Cineraria
Large, colourful, daisy-like flowers in massed heads from early winter to early summer. Varieties in many colours.
Propagation: Seeds (pp. 30/31).

• **Sparmannia africana**
African Hemp/House Lime
Heart-shaped, bright green leaves covered with soft hairs. White flowers from late spring to early summer.
Propagation: Cuttings (pp. 42/43).

PLANTS NEEDING CARE

• **Aglaoenema modestum**
Chinese Evergreen
Long, spear-shaped leaves. Many other species, some with attractively variegated leaves.
Propagation: Division (pp. 34/35) and removal of basal shoots in spring.

• **Aphelandra squarrosa**
Saffron Plant/Zebra Plant
Oval and pointed, dark green leaves with ivory veins. Cone-shaped heads formed of yellow flowers appear from mid to late summer.
Propagation: Cuttings (pp. 42/43).

• **Dieffenbacia maculata**
(syn. *D. picta*)
Dumb Cane/Leopard Lily/Spotted Dumb Cane
Large, oblong leaves in many colours. Avoid contact with the sap. Many colourful varieties.
Propagation: Cane cuttings (pp. 58/59).

• **Bromeliads**
Wide range of distinctive plants, many with leaves forming urns, including genera *Aechmea, Ananas, Cryptanthus, Guzmania, Neoregelia* and *Vriesia.*
Propagation: Division (pp. 34/35) and removal of offsets.

• **Ctenanthe oppenheimiana tricolor**
Never Never Plant
Narrow, lance-shaped leaves with dark green and grey bands.
Propagation: Division (pp. 34/35).

• **Maranta leuconeura**
Prayer Plant/Ten Commandments
Oval, emerald-green leaves, blotched in purple-brown, that stand upright at

Cissus antarctica – Kangaroo Vine

night, as if in prayer. Several attractive varieties.
Propagation: Division (pp. 34/35).

• **Pilea cadierei**
Aluminium Plant/Watermelon Pilea
Oval and pointed, mid-green, quilted leaves with silvery patches.
Propagation: Cuttings (pp. 42/43).

• **Rhoeo spathacea**
(syn. *Rhoeo discolor*)
Fleshy, lance-shaped, glossy-green leaves with purplish undersides.
Propagation: Division (pp. 34/35) and Cuttings (pp. 42/43) from basal shoots in spring.

PLANTS WITH A CHALLENGE

• **Acalypha hispida**
Chenille Plant/Fox Tail/Philippine Medusa/Red Cat Tail/Red-hot Catstail
Long, tail-like stems packed with red flowers during summer and into autumn.
Propagation: Cuttings (pp. 42/43).

• **Anthurium andreanum**
Flamingo Lily/Oilcloth Flower/Painter's Palette
Large, heart-shaped leaves and waxy

red spathes from which arise straight columns of flowers.
Propagation: Division (pp. 34/35).
• *Anthurium crystallinum*
Crystal Anthurium/Strap Flower
Large, heart-shaped, velvet-surfaced, dark green leaves with attractive ivory veins.
Propagation: Division (pp. 34/35).
• *Anthurium scherzerianum*
Flamingo Flower/Pigtail Anthurium/Pigtail Plant
Dark green, lance-shaped leaves and red spathes with curly, orange-red columns.
Propagation: Division (pp. 34/35).
• *Caladium hortulanum*
Angel's Wings/Elephant's Ears/Mother-in-law Plant
Large, arrow-shaped, paper-thin leaves with many attractive colours.
Propagation: Remove and pot-up offsets in spring.
• *Calathea makoyana*
(syn. *Maranta makcyana*)
Brain Plant/Cathedral Windows/Peacock Plant
Oblong, paper-thin leaves, silvery-green above and attractively patterned.
Propagation: Division (pp. 34/35).

Ficus lyrata – Fiddle-leaf Fig

• *Pachystachys lutea*
Lollipop Plant
Cone-shaped heads of bright yellow flowers from late spring to autumn.
Propagation: Cuttings (pp. 42/43).
• *Spathiphyllum wallisii*
Peace Lily/Spathe Flower
Spear-shaped, glossy-green leaves and white, arum-like flowers on long, upright stems from late spring to mid summer.
Propagation: Division (pp. 34/35).

OTHER PLANTS TO CONSIDER

EASY TO GROW
• *Achimenes hybrida* (pp. 96/97)
• *Asparagus densiflorus* 'Meyeri' (pp. 100/101)
• *Asparagus densiflorus* 'Sprengeri' (pp. 100/101)
• *Campanula isophylla* (pp. 94/95)
• *Chlorophytum comosum* (pp. 100/101)
• *Cissus antarctica* (pp. 98/99)
• *Cissus rhombifolia* (pp. 98/99)
• *Cissus rhombifolia* 'Ellen Danica' (pp. 98/99)
• *Cyperus alternifolius* (pp. 102/103)
• *Glechoma hederacea* 'Variegata' (pp. 100/101)
• *Hedera canariensis* 'Variegata' (pp. 100/101)
• *Hedera helix* (pp. 98/99)
• *Hyacinthus orientalis* (pp. 98/99)
• *Mikania ternata* (pp. 100/101)
• *Nephrolepis exaltata* (pp. 100/101)
• *Nephrolepis exaltata* 'Bostoniensis' (pp. 100/101)
• *Pellaea rotundifolia* (pp. 100/101)
• *Plectranthus australis* (pp. 100/101)
• *Plectranthus coleoides* 'Marginatus' (pp. 100/101)
• *Plectranthus oertendahlii* (pp. 100/101)
• *Saxifraga stolonifera* 'Tricolor' (pp. 100/101)
• *Schizocentron elegans* (pp. 94/95)
• *Senecio macroglossus* 'Variegatus' (pp. 98/99)
• *Senecio mikanioides* (pp. 98/99)
• *Soleirolia soleirolii* (pp. 100/101)

PLANTS NEEDING CARE
• *Araucaria heterophylla* (pp. 102/103)

Hyacinthus orientalis – Hyacinth

• *Ardisia crenata* (pp. 102/103 and 108/109)
• *Begonia limmingheana* (pp. 94/95)
• *Begonia tuberhybrida* 'Pendula' (pp. 94/95)
• *Brassaia actinophylla* (pp. 102/103)
• *Clerodendrum thomsoniae* (pp. 96/97)
• *Cyclamen persicum* (pp. 104/105)
• *Dionaea muscipula* (pp. 106/107)
• *Dizygotheca elegantissima* (pp. 102/103)
• *Epipremnum pinnatum* 'Aureum' (98/99 and 100/101)
• *Ficus benjamina* (pp. 102/103)
• *Ficus deltoidea* (pp. 102/103 and 108/109)
• *Ficus elastica* (pp. 102/103)
• *Ficus lyrata* (pp. 102/103)
• *Gloriosa rothschildiana* (pp. 96/97)
• *Gloriosa superba* (pp. 96/97)
• *Gynura aurantiaca* (pp. 100/101)
• *Gynura procumbens* (pp. 100/101)
• *Monstera deliciosa* (pp. 98/99 and 102/103)
• *Philodendron domesticum* (pp. 98/99)
• *Philodendron erubescens* (pp. 98/99)
• *Phoenix canariensis* (pp. 102/103)
• *Piper crocatum* (pp. 98/99)
• *Saintpaulia grotei* (pp. 94/95)
• *Schefflera arboricola* (pp. 102/103)

PLANTS WITH A CHALLENGE
• *Aeschynanthus radicans* (pp. 94/95)
• *Aeschynanthus speciosus* (pp. 94/95)
• *Cestrum parqui* (pp. 104/105)
• *Columnea banksii* (pp. 94/95)
• *Columnea gloriosa* (pp. 94/95)
• *Columnea microphylla* (pp. 94/95)
• *Darlingtonia californica* (pp. 106/107)
• *Dipladenia sanderi* 'Rosea' (pp. 96/97)
• *Dracaena deremensis* (pp. 102/103)
• *Drosera binata* (pp. 106/107)
• *Drosera capensis* (pp. 106/107)
• *Episcia cupreata* (pp. 94/95)
• *Episcia dianthiflora* (pp. 94/95)
• *Fittonia verschaffeltii* (pp. 100/101)
• *Fittonia verschaffeltii* 'Argyroneura' (PP. 100/101)
• *Fittonia verschaffeltii* 'Argyroneura Nana' (pp. 100/101)
• *Gardenia jasminoides* (pp. 104/105)
• *Hoya bella* (pp. 94/95 and 104/105)
• *Hoya carnosa* (pp. 96/97 and 104/105)
• *Philodendron melanochrysum* (pp. 98/99)
• *Pittosporum tobira* (pp. 104/105)
• *Sarracenia flava* (pp. 106/107)
• *Sarracenia purpurea* (pp. 106/107)
• *Stephanotis floribunda* (pp. 96/97 and 104/105)

No plant will indefinitely survive in total shade, although some grow in shade near a sunless window or where the light is just sufficient to enable a newspaper to be read. If a plant appears sickly, move it to better light to encourage recovery.

Because of the inherent difficulties in growing houseplants in little light, those that are difficult to grow cease to be possible options and therefore most are either easy to grow, or present only a slight degree of difficulty. Also, some plants that are moderately easy to grow in moderate light become a challenge when the intensity of light falls. Remember that the intensity of light 2.4m/8ft from a window is only 5-10% of that on a windowsill.

Many of the plants recommended for growing in soft light can also be grown in slight shade for a limited time.

IF IT'S TOO DARK ...

- stems and leaves turn towards the light, although plants can be given a quarter of a turn every few days to ensure upright growth.
- variegated plants lose their rich colouring and become green.
- new leaves become smaller, and paler.
- lower leaves become yellow, eventually falling off.
- shoots become spindly, with long spaces between leaf-joints.
- flowers cease to develop.

EASY TO GROW
- *Aspidistra elatior*
Barroom Plant/Cast Iron Plant
Long, lance-shaped, dark green leaves. The variegated form needs better light than the all-green type.
Propagation: Division (pp. 34/35).
- *Asplenium bulbiferum*
Hen-and-chicken Fern/King and Queen Fern/Mother Fern/Mother Spleenwort
Finely-cut, mid-green leaves. Small bulbils arise from their upper surfaces, and can be easily rooted.
Propagation: Division (pp. 34/35) and bulbils (pp. 40/41).
- *Cyrtomium falcatum*

Syngonium podophyllum – Arrowhead Vine

Fishtail Fern/Holly Fern/Japanese Holly Fern

Holly-like, stiff, glossy, dark-green leaflets.

Propagation: Division (pp. 34/35).

PLANTS NEEDING CARE

- ***Dracaena fragrans***
Corn Plant
Long, sword-like leaves: attractive varieties have white or silver stripes along the green leaves.
Propagation: Cane cuttings (pp. 58/59) and removal and potting up of basal shoots in spring.
- ***Dracaena marginata***
Madagascar Dragon Tree
Narrow, sword-like green leaves with red edges.

Propagation: Cane cuttings (pp. 58/58) and removal and potting up of basal shoots in spring.

OTHER PLANTS TO CONSIDER

EASY TO GROW

- *Ficus pumila* (pp. 100/101)
- *Philodendron scandens* (pp. 98/99 and 100/101)

PLANTS NEEDING CARE

- *Cissus discolor* (pp. 98/99)
- *Howeia belmoreana* (pp. 102/103)
- *Howeia forsteriana* (pp. 102/103)
- *Syngonium podophyllum* (pp. 98/99) – but the variegated varieties need soft light.

Cissus discolor – Begonia Vine

Ficus pumila 'Sonny' – Creeping Fig

Glossary of Terms

Acaricide: A chemical used to kill parasitic spider mites. Houseplants, especially those in dry, warm sunrooms, conservatories and greenhouses, are likely to be attacked by red spider mites.

Acid: Refers to soils and composts with a pH below 7.0. Most plants grow best in slightly acid conditions, about 6.5.

Activator: A chemical product, normally granular or powdered, that speeds up the decay of plant material in a compost heap.

Adventitious roots: Roots appearing in an unusual position, such as on leaves and stems.

Aerial roots: Roots that appear from a stem above soil-level, as with some Ivies (*Hedera*) and orchids. The Swiss Cheese Plant (*Monstera deliciosa*), as well as some philodendrons, has aerial roots.

Air layering: A method of increasing certain plants by encouraging roots to form on stems. The Rubber Plant (*Ficus elastica*) is a plant often increased in this way.

Alkaline: Refers to soils with a pH above 7.0.

Alpine: Generally refers to any small plant grown in a rock garden or alpine house, but strictly a plant that in its natural habitat grows on mountains, above the level at which trees thrive.

Alpine house: An unheated greenhouse where alpine plants can be grown. The house's structure enables air to circulate freely around plants.

Alternate: Buds or leaves that grow on opposite sides of a stem, but in positions not directly opposite one another.

Annual: A plant that completes its life-cycle within one year: seeds germinate, the plant grows and flowers are produced, which in their turn produce seed. However, many plants that are not strictly annuals are treated as such. For instance, the Marvel of Peru (*Mirabilis jalapa*) is a perennial grown as a half-hardy annual, and Busy Lizzie (*Impatiens walleriana*) is a greenhouse perennial cultivated as a half-hardy annual.

Anther: Part of a stamen, the male reproductive part of a flower. A stamen is formed of a stalk (filament) with an anther at its top. Pollen grains are contained in the anther.

Aphids: Perhaps the best-known pest of plants, also called greenfly and blackfly. They breed rapidly during spring and summer, clustering around flowers, shoots, stems and leaves. They suck the sap, causing debilitation as well as spreading viruses.

Apical: The tip of a branch or shoot.

Aquatic: A plant that grows partly or entirely in water.

Areole: A modified sideshoot, resembling a tiny hump, unique to cacti. It bears spines, hairs, bristles or wool.

Aroid: A plant belonging to the Arum Family and including Anthuriums, Dieffenbachias, Monsteras and Philodendrons.

Asexual: Non-sexual and frequently used to refer to the vegetative propagation of plants, such as by cuttings and division.

Axil: The junction between a leaf and stem, from where sideshoots or flowers may develop.

Axillary: A bud that grows from an axil, later forming a stem and flowers, or just a stem. Some flowers have their sideshoots removed to encourage the development of larger blooms.

Bearded: A petal bearing a tuft or row of long hairs.

Bedding plant: A plant raised and used as a temporary filler in a border. Spring-bedding plants are planted in autumn for spring flowering and include wallflowers and tulips, while summer-bedding plants are planted in spring for summer flowering. Usually, half-hardy annuals are raised under glass early in the year so that they are well established when planted.

Biennial: A plant that makes its initial growth one year and flowers the following one. However, many plants not strictly biennial by nature are grown as biennials. For instance, the

Common Daisy (*Bellis perennis*) and Sweet William (*Dianthus barbatus*) are perennials usually grown as a biennials.

Bigeneric hybrid: A plant produced by crossing two plants from different genera. This is indicated by a cross positioned in front of the plant's name. For instance, the Ivy Tree (*X Fatshedera lizei*) is a cross between a form of the False Castor Oil Plant (*Fatsia japonica* 'Moseri'), also known as the Japanese Fatsia, and the Irish Ivy (*Hedera helix* 'Hibernica').

Bleeding: The loss of sap from plants after they have been cut.

Blind: A plant whose growing point has not developed properly.

Bloom: This has two meanings – either a flower or a powdery coating.

Bolting: The premature shooting up to flower of vegetables. Lettuces, beetroot, spinach and radishes are most susceptible.

Bonsai: The art of growing dwarfed shrubs and trees in small containers. The plants are kept small by restricting their roots, pruning leaves and shoots, and trimming roots. Outdoor bonsai plants are not true houseplants, and can only be taken indoors for limited periods. Indoor bonsai plants, however, remain perpetually indoors.

Botrytis: Also known as grey mould, a fungal disease prevalent in badly ventilated, damp sunrooms, greenhouses and conservatories. Soft-tissued plants such as lettuces and delicately flowered types like chrysanthemums are particularly susceptible to it.

Bordeaux mixture: A fungicidal mixture of copper sulphate and lime.

Bottle gardening: Growing plants in enclosed environments created by large glass jars, such as carboys.

Bottom heat: The warming from below of a rooting mixture, rather than from above. The warmth is usually provided by electric cables buried under a layer of well-drained and aerated rooting compost. Cuttings inserted into this root rapidly and seeds in boxes or pots

placed on top are encouraged to germinate quickly. In early days, bottom heat was supplied by hot water pipes or the fermentation of manure.

Bract: A modified leaf and usually associated with flowers. Some act as protection for the flower, while others appear to take the place of petals and to be the main attraction. Poinsettias (*Euphorbia pulcherrima*), for instance, have brightly coloured bracts that dominate the flowers.

Break: The branching of shoots after the removal of a terminal bud. The term breaking is also used to describe streaking and flaking of another colour in some flowers, usually caused by a virus.

Bromeliad: A member of the *Bromeliaceae* family. Many have rosettes of leaves and colourful bracts, and a few are epiphytes.

Bud: A tightly-packed and enclosed immature shoot or flower.

Bulb: A storage organ with a bud-like structure. It is formed of fleshy scales attached at their bases to a flattened stem called the basal plate. Tulips and hyacinths are examples of bulbs. Erroneously, the term is often collectively used to include tubers, rhizomes and corms.

Bulbil: An immature and miniature bulb, usually at the base of another bulb. However, some plants, such as the Mother Fern (*Asplenium bulbiferum*), also known as the Hen-and-Chickens Fern, develop plantlets on their leaves that are known as bulbils. These can be used to increase the plant.

Cactus: A succulent plant belonging to the *Cactaceae* family. All cactus plants are characterized by having areoles.

Calcicole: A plant that likes lime.

Calcifuge: A plant that does not like lime.

Calyx: The sepals as a whole; the outer ring of a flower.

Capillary action: The passage of water upwards through soil or potting compost. The finer the soil particles, the higher the rise of moisture. The same principle is used in self-watering systems for plants in pots in sunrooms, conservatories and greenhouse.

Carboy: A large, somewhat round or pear-shaped glass bottle used as a container for plants.

Catch crop: A crop – usually of a salad nature and sometimes raised in greenhouses – that is sown, grown and harvested while situated between long-growing crops.

Chestnut compound: A mixture of copper sulphate and ammonium carbonate to control some fungal diseases.

Chlorophyll: The green pigment present in all plants, except for a few parasites and fungi. It absorbs energy from the sun and plays a vital role in photosynthesis, the process by which plants grow.

Chlorosis: A disorder mainly of leaves, with parts becoming light-coloured or whitish. It has several causes: viruses, mutation or through mineral deficiency. The variegated, speckled or mottled colouring in some plants is not always the result of hybridization or selection, but of a virus.

Cloche: The French for a bell-glass, but now widely used for glass and plastic tunnel-like structures used to protect early-maturing crops, usually vegetables.

Cladode: A modified, flattened stem which takes the form and function of a leaf.

Clone: A plant raised vegetatively from another plant, so that it is identical in every particular to other plants raised from the same plant.

Columnar: A plant that rises vertically – usually used to refer to trees and conifers, but also to describe some cacti.

Compost: Has two meanings. The first refers to the medium in which plants grow when in pots or other containers, and in North America is known as potting soil. It is formed of either a mixture of loam, sharp sand and peat, plus fertilizers, or mainly peat and usually known as peat-based compost. The other meaning is the material produced after the total decay of vegetable waste. This is applied to soil as a substitute for farmyard manure, dug into the soil or spread over the surface as a mulch.

Compound leaf: A leaf formed of two or more leaflets. Compound leaves are characterized by not having buds in the axils of their leaflets. All true leaves have buds in their axils.

Corm: An underground storage organ formed of a greatly swollen stem base, such as a gladiolus. Young corms – cormlets – form around the bases of corms, and can be removed and grown in a nursery bed for several seasons before reaching the size of a flowering corm.

Corolla: The ring of petals in a flower, creating the main display.

Corona: The development of petals in certain plants to form a cup or trumpet, as in daffodils.

Cristate: Crested – used to describe some ferns and cacti, as well as a few forms of houseplants.

Crock: A piece of broken clay pot put in the base of a pot to prevent the drainage hole being blocked by compost.

Crown buds: The buds on chrysanthemums that develop after the plant had been initially stopped (having the terminal bud removed).

Cultivar: A variety raised in cultivation by selective breeding.

Cutting: A vegetative method of increasing plants, by which a severed piece of the parent plant is encouraged to develop roots.

Damping down: A method of increasing the humidity in a sunroom, conservatory or greenhouse. Use a fine-rose watering-can and clean water to dampen the floor and staging, mainly in summer. It is best carried out early in the day so that excess moisture dries before nightfall. Take care that the atmosphere is not damp at night.

Damping off: A disease that usually attacks seedlings soon after germination. It is encouraged by overcrowding, a stuffy atmosphere and bad drainage in the compost.

Dead heading: The removal of faded and dead flowers to encourage the development of further flowers. It also helps to keep plants tidy and prevents diseases attacking dead and decaying flowers.

Deciduous: A plant that loses its leaves at the begining of winter and produces a new set at the onset of spring.

Derris: A pesticide (better known in North America as Rotenone) for killing pests on plants.

Dibber: A rounded, blunt-pointed tool for making planting holes. Large dibbers are used to plant brassicas and other members of the cabbage family, while small ones are for pricking off seedlings into boxes or pots of compost.

Dieback: The death of part of a stem, often caused by faulty pruning or the removal of cuttings.

Disbudding: The removal of buds from around the sides of a main, central bud to encourage the development of one flower.

Division: A vegetative method of propagation involving dividing the roots of plants.

Dormancy: The resting period of a plant or seed.

Double flowers: Flowers with more than the normal number of petals in their formation.

Downy mildew: A fungal disease resulting from cool, damp conditions.

Drawn: Thin and spindly shoots, after being in crowded or dark conditions.

Dutch light: A large piece of glass secured in a wooden frame and used to protect plants. Often, half-hardy bedding plants – earlier raised in the warmth of a greenhouse – are acclimatized to outside conditions by placing them under a Dutch light.

Epiphyte: A plant that grows above ground-level, attached to trees, rocks and, sometimes, to other plants. These plants do not take nourishment from their host, but just use them for support. Many orchids and bromeliads are epiphytes.

Etiolated: Blanched and spindly – the result of being grown in poor light.

Evergreen: A plant that retains its leaves throughout the year.

Exotic: A plant introduced from abroad. Usually used to refer to plants from tropical and sub-tropical regions.

Eye: The centre of a flower – often having a different colour from the rest of the bloom.

F1: The first filial generation – the result of a cross between two pure-bred parents. F1 hybrids are large and strong plants, but their seeds will not produce replicas of the parents.

Fasciation: A freak condition when stems or flowers are fused and flattened. Fasciated parts are best cut out.

Fern: A perennial, flowerless plant that produces spores.

Fertilization: The sexual union of the male cell (pollen) and the female cell (ovule). Fertilization may be the result of pollination, when pollen falls upon the stigma. However, not all pollen germinates after falling on a stigma.

Fertilize: To encourage the development of a plant by feeding it with chemicals or manure.

Filament: The slender stalk that supports the anthers of a flower. Collectively, the anthers and filaments are the stamen.

Fimbriated: Fringed – usually applied to a flower or petal.

Flore-pleno: Refers to flowers that have a larger than normal number of petals.

Floret: A small flower that with others forms a flower head, such as in chrysanthemums and other members of the Compositae family.

Flower: Usually, the most attractive and eye-catching part of a plant. It usually contains both the male and female reproductive parts, although some flowers have just male organs, and others are formed only of female parts. The most attractive parts are usually the petals.

Foliar feed: A fertilizer applied to foliage.

Forcing: Encouraging a plant to bear flowers or come to maturity before its natural season.

Frame: A low structure formed of brick or wood, with a glass covering of Dutch lights. An invaluable part of greenhouse gardening, enabling seedlings and plants to be hardened off before being planted in a garden.

Frond: The leaf of a palm or fern.

Fungicide: A chemical to combat fungal diseases.

Genus: A group of plants with similar botanical characteristics. Some genera (plural of genus) contain many species, other just one and are then said to be monotypic.

Germination: The process that occurs within a seed when given moisture, air and warmth. The coat of the seed ruptures and a seed leaf (or leaves) grows towards the light. A root develops at the same time. However, to most gardeners, germination is when they see shoots appearing through the surface of potting compost or soil.

Glaucous: Greyish-green or bluish-green in colour – usually applied to the stems, leaves or fruits of ornamental plants.

Glochid: A small hooked hair growing on some cacti.

Growing point: The terminal part of a stem or shoot that creates extension growth. Also known as the growing tip.

Half-hardy: A plant that can withstand fairly low temperatures, but needs protection from frost. For example, half-hardy annuals are raised in warmth in a greenhouse early in the year and subsequently planted out into a garden as soon as all risk of frost has passed.

Hardening off: The gradual accustoming of

plants to outside conditions. This especially applies to plants propagated in greenhouses in late winter and early spring for later planting into a garden.

Hardy: A plant hardy enough to survive outside throughout the year, even in areas where the temperature falls below freezing. Some hardy plants, such as *Aucuba japonica* 'Variegata', are grown as houseplants.

Heel: A hard, corky layer of bark and stem remaining at the base of a sideshoot after it has been gently pulled from a stem. Some cuttings root quickly if this area remains. However, torn edges from around its sides must be trimmed. Cuttings taken in this way are called heel cuttings.

Herbaceous: A plant that dies down to soil-level in autumn and develops fresh growth during the following spring.

Hermaphrodite: Having both male and female organs in the same flower.

Honeydew: A sugary and sticky material excreted by aphids and other sap-sucking insects. Often, fungus moulds grow upon it, creating a black, unsightly mess.

Hormone: A growth-regulating chemical that occurs naturally in both plant and animal tissue. Synthetic hormones are widely used to encourage cuttings to develop roots quickly.

Humus: Wholly or partly decomposed vegetable material.

Hybrid: Progeny from parents of different species or genera.

Hybridization: The crossing of one or more generations of plants to improve a wide range of characteristics, such as flower size, time of flowering and sturdiness.

Hydroculture: The growing of plants without the aid of soil. It is also known as hydroponics.

Incurved: Petals that curl inwards. Some chrysanthemums have incurved flowers.

Inflorescence: Part of a plant that bears flowers.

Insecticide: A chemical used to kill insects.

Insectiverous: A plant that is adapted to trap, kill and digest insects.

Internodal: The part on a stem or shoot between two leaf-joints (nodes).

Joint: The junction of a shoot and stem, or a leaf and leaf-stalk. Frequently, these are known as nodes.

Juvenile leaf: Several plants grown as houseplants have, when young, differently shaped leaves from those on mature plants. For instance, when young the False Aralia (*Dizygotheca elegantissima*) has long, wavy-edged leaves. In mature specimens, these broaden and lose their delicate and lacy appearance.

Layering: A vegetative method of increasing plants, involving lowering stems and slightly burying them in soil or compost. By creating a kink, twist, bend or slit in the stem, the flow of sap is restricted and roots induced to develop.

Leaf: A structure (wide range of shapes and sizes) borne on the aerial part of a plant, and having a bud in its axil.

Leaflet: Some leaves are formed of several small leaves (leaflets), characterized by not having buds in their individual axils.

Leaf margin: The edge of a leaf.

Leggy: Plants that become tall and spindly, often through being kept in dark places.

Lime: An alkaline material used to counteract acidity in the soil and improve clay soils by encouraging small particles to group together increasing its drainage and aeration properties.

Loam: A mixture of fertile soil – formed of sand, clay, silt and organic material.

Midrib: The central or main vein on a leaf or leaflet.

Mildew: A fungal disease that attacks soft-tissued plants.

Mist propagation: A mechanical device that sprays fine droplets of water over cuttings. This keeps the cuttings cool, as well as reducing their need to absorb moisture before the development of roots.

Mutation: Part of a plant – usually the flower – that differs from the plant's normal characteristics.

Neutral: Neither acid nor alkaline. Chemically, neutral on the pH scale is 7.0, but horticulturally neutral is considered to be between 6.5 and 7.0.

Node: A leaf joint or position where a shoot grows from a stem or main branch.

Offset: A shoot arising from the base of a plant, often just below compost level. It can be detached and encouraged to develop roots. Many bromeliads are increased in this manner.

Opposite: Buds or leaves borne in pairs along shoots and stems.

Organic: The cultivation of plants without the use of chemical fertilizers or pesticides.

Ovary: The part of a flower in which seeds are formed.

Peat: Partly decayed vegetable material, usually with an acid nature. Becauseof its high capacity to retain water, it is often used in potting composts.

Perennial: Usually used when referring to herbaceous perennials, but also applied to any plant that lives for several years, including trees, shrubs and climbers.

Pesticide: A chemical compound for killing insects and other pests.

Petal: Usually the most attractive and showy part of a flower. Petals both protect the reproductive parts of the flower, and attract pollinating insects.

Petiole: A leaf-stalk.

Photosynthesis: Food-building process when chlorophyll in the leaves is activated by sunlight. It reacts with moisture absorbed by roots, and carbon-dioxide gained from the atmosphere, to create growth.

Phototropism: The action on a plant that makes it grow towards a light source.

pH: A logarithmic scale used to define the acidity or alkalinity of a soil-water solution. Chemically, neutral is 7.0, with figures above indicating increasing alkalinity, and below increasing acidity. Most plants grow well in 6.5-7.0.

Pinching out: Removal of the tip of a shoot, or a terminal bud, to encourage the development of sideshoots.

Pip: Two distinct meanings – the seed of some fruits, such as apples and pears, and the rootstock of plants like Lily of the Valley (*Convallaria majalis*).

Plantlet: An offset produced on a plant's leaves or stems.

Plunging: The placing outdoors of plants or bulbs in pots and covering to the rim with peat, ashes or garden soil.

Pollen: The male fertilizing agent from the anthers.

Pot bound: When a plant fills its pot with roots and requires repotting into a larger container.

Potting mix: The potting compost in which plants are grown.

Potting-on: The transfer of an established plant from one pot to a larger one.

Potting soil: The American term for potting compost.

Potting-up: The transfer of a young plant from a seedbox or seed-pan into a pot.

Pricking-out: The transfer of seedlings from a seedbox or seed-pan into another box, where they can be given more space.

Propagation: The raising of new plants.

Pseudobulb: The thickened stem of an orchid plant.

Rhizome: An underground or partly buried horizontal stem. They can be slender or fleshy.

Ring culture: A method of growing tomatoes in bottomless pots on a base of well-drained gravel.

Root ball: The potting compost in which a houseplant grows, together with the roots.

Root hair: Feeding hairs that develop on roots to absorb nutrients.

Rosette: A crowded and circular cluster of leaves.

Scree: A freely-draining area of grit and small stones for alpine plants.

Seed: A fertilized, ripened ovule.

Seed leaf: The first leaf (sometimes two) that appears after germination.

Seedling: A young plant produced after a seed germinates. It has a single, unbranched stem.

Self-coloured: Flowers that are just one colour, as opposed to bicoloured (two colours) or multicoloured (several colours).

Sequestrene: A chemical compound enabling plants to absorb minerals locked up in some soils.

Sessile: Leaves and flowers that do not have stalks or stems attaching them to the plant.

Sideshoot: A shoot growing out from the side of a main shoot or stem.

Single flowers: These have the normal number of petals, arranged in a single row.

Softwood cutting: A cutting formed from a non-woody shoot.

Spadix: A dense spike of tiny flowers, usually enclosed in a spathe.

Spathe: A bract or pair of bracts – often brightly coloured and dominant – that enclose flowers, as in members of the Arum family.

Species: A group of plants that breed together and have the same characteristics.

Spores: The reproductive cells of non-flowering plants, such as ferns.

Sport: A plant that reveals a marked difference from its parent. It is also known as a mutation.

Stamen: The male part of a flower.

Sterilization: The cleansing of soil, killing weed seeds, fungi and bacteria, by heat or chemicals.

Stigma: The female part of a flower.

Stipule: Leaf-like sheaths at the bases of some flower stalks.

Stoma: Minute holes – usually on the undersides of leaves – that enable the exchange of gases between the plant and surrounding air. During respiration, plants absorb air, retaining and using oxygen and giving off carbon dioxide. However, during photosynthesis plants absorbs air, using the carbon dioxide and giving off oxygen. The singular of stoma is stomata.

Stool: Usually refers to chrysanthemum plants when cut down after flowering to 10-15cm/4-6in high. These stools are stored in a cool place throughout winter and in spring encouraged to produce shoots, later used as cuttings.

Stop: Removal of a growing tip to encourage the development of sideshoots.

Stove plant: A plant that requires a high temperature.

Strain: Seed-raised plants from a common ancestor.

Strike: The rooting of a cutting.

Style: Part of the female reproductive element of a flower, linking the stigma to the ovary.

Sucker: Shoots that develop from the roots of a plant, forming their own leaves and roots.

Succulent: Any plant with thick and fleshy leaves. Cacti are succulent plants, but not all succulents are cacti.

Synonym: A previous botanical name for a plant. It frequently happens that a plant is better known and sold by nurseries under an earlier name.

Systemic: Chemicals that enter a plant's tissue, killing sucking or biting insects. The period these chemicals remain active within a plant depends on the type of plant, the temperature and the chemical.

Tender: A plant that is not hardy, and which is likely to be damaged by low temperatures.

Tendril: A thread-like growth that enables some climbers to cling to their supports.

Terrarium: A glass container that is partly or wholly enclosed and used to house plants.

Terrestrial: Plants that grow in soil at ground-level.

Topdressing: The removal of soil from the surface of plants in large containers, replacing it with fresh potting compost. Plants are normally topdressed because they are too large to be repotted into fresh compost in a larger pot.

Transpiration: The loss of moisture from a plant.

Tuber: An underground storage organ, such as that of a dahlia.

Turgid: Used to describe plants that are firm and full of water.

Variegated: Multi-coloured leaves.

Variety: A naturally occurring variation of a species. However, the term variety is commonly used to include both true varieties and cultivars. Cultivars are plants that are variations of a species and have been raised in cultivation.

Vegetative propagation: A method of increasing plants, including the division of roots, layering, grafting, budding and taking cuttings.

Index

A

Acalypha hispida 112
Achimenes hybrida 96, 113
Aeschynanthus pulcher 94
Aeschynanthus radicans 94, 113
Aeschynanthus speciosus 94, 113
African Evergreen 99
African Hemp 112
Aglaonema modestum 111
Algerian Ivy 98
Allamanda cathartica 'Grandiflora' 96, 111
Alsobia dianthiflora 95
Aluminium Plant 112
Amaryllis 110
Angel's Tears 101
Angel's Wings 113
Anthurium andreanum 112
Anthurium crystallinum 113
Anthurium scherzerianum 113
Aphelandra squarrosa 111
Aphids 84
Aporocactus flagelliformis 94, 111
Arabian Violet 104
Aralia elegantissima 102
Araucaria excelsa 102
Araucaria heterophylla 102, 113
Architectural plants 102
Ardisia crenata 102, 104, 108, 113
Ardisia crenulata 102, 104, 108
Ardisia crispa 102, 104, 108
Arrowhead Vine 99
Artillery Plant 111
Asparagus densiflorus 'Meyeri' 100, 113
Asparagus densiflorus 'Sprengeri' 100, 113
Asparagus Fern 100
Asparagus meyeri 100
Asparagus sprengeri 100
Assam Rubber 102
Aspidistra elatior 114
Asplenium bulbiferum 114
Astilbe japonica 110
Aucuba japonica 'Maculata' 110
Aucuba japonica 'Variegata' 110
Australian Laurel 105
Australian Pine 102
Azalea 111

B

Baby Primrose 104
Baby's Tears 101
Bag Flower 96
Barbados Lily 110
Barroom Plant 114
Basket Begonia 94
Basket Vine 100

Bead Plant 108
Beaver's Tail 101
Beefsteak Plant 110
Begonia glaucophylla 94
Begonia limmingheana 94, 113
Begonia masoniana 112
Begonia rex 112
Begonia tuberhybrida pendula 94, 113
Begonia Vine 99
Belmore Sentry Palm 103
Beloperone guttata 111
Benjamin Tree 102
Berried houseplants 108
Black-eyed Susan 96
Black Gold Philodendron 99
Black leg 89
Blacking Plant 111
Bleeding Heart 96
Blood Leaf 110
Blue Passion Flower 97
Blushing Philodendron 99
Bonsai 74-79
    Chinese 74, 79
    indoor 74, 79
    Japanese 74, 79
    looking after 77, 78
    outdoor 74, 79
    pruning 78
    repotting 74-76
    root pruning 74-76
    suitable plants 79
        indoor types 79
        outdoor types 79
    tools required 74
    wiring 79
Boston Fern 100
Botrytis 88
Bottle garden, planting 66, 67
    looking after 67
    suitable plants 66
Bougainvillea glabra 96, 111
Bougainvillea 'Mrs. Butt' 96, 111
Bowstring Hemp 110
Brain Plant 113
Brassaia actinophylla 102, 113
Brazilian Coleus 101
Bromeliads 112
Bulbs and corms 60-65
    after flowering 61
Burro's Tail 101
Busy Lizzie 110
Busy Lizzy 110
Butterfly Flower 110
Button Fern 100
Buying houseplants 12, 13

C

Cacti (Desert types) 110
Caladium hortulanum 113
Calamondin Orange 108
Calathea makoyana 113
Calceolaria x herbeohybrida 112
Calceolaria x hybrida 112
Californian Pitcher Plant 106
Callisia elegans 100, 111
Campanula isophylla 94, 113
Canary Date Palm 103
Canary Island Date 103
Canary Island Ivy 98
Cape Ivy 99
Cape Jasmine 105
Cape Leadwort 97
Capsicum annuum 108, 111
Cast Iron Plant 114
Carboy, planting 66, 67
Carpet Plant 101
Cathedral Windows 113
Celosia argentea cristata 110
Celosia cristata 110
Cereus flagelliformis 94
Ceropegia woodii 101, 111
Cestrum parqui 105, 113
Chenille Plant 112
Chilli 108
China Rose 111
Chinese Dwarf Lemon 109
Chinese Evergreen 111
Chinese Hibiscus 111
Chlorophytum comosum 100, 113
Christmas Cactus 94
Christmas Flower 111
Christmas Pepper 108
Christmas Star 111
Chrysamphora californica 106
Chrysanthemum 110
Cineraria 112
Cineraria cruenta 112
Cissus antarctica 98, 113
Cissus discolor 99, 115
Cissus rhombifolia 98, 113
Cissus rhombifolia 'Ellen Danica' 98, 113
Citrofortunella mitis 108, 111
Citrus limon 'Meyeri' 109, 111
Citrus meyeri 109
Citrus mitis 108
Claw Cactus 94
Clerodendrum thomsoniae 96, 113
Climbing Begonia 99
Climbing Fig 100
Climbing foliage plants 98
Climbing Lily 97

Cobra Lily 106
Cobra Orchid 106
Cockscomb 110
Codiaeum variegatum pictum 111
Coleus blumei 110
Columnea x banksii 95,
Columnea gloriosa 95, 113
Columnea microphylla 95, 113
Common Allamanda 96
Common Ivy 98
Common Passion Flower 97
Composts 14, 15
    loam-based 15
    peat-based 15
Coral Berry 102, 104, 108
Cordyline fruticosa 111
Cordyline terminalis 111
Corn Plant 115
Corsican Carpet Plant 101
Crab Cactus 94
Creeping Fig 100
Creeping Rubber Plant 100
Creeping Sailor 101
Crocuses 64
    potting 64
Croton 111
Crystal Anthurium 113
Ctenanthe oppenhiemiana tricolor 112
Cupid Peperomia 101
Cupid's Bower 96
Curly Palm 103
Cyclamen 104
Cyclamen mites 86
Cyclamen persicum 104, 113
Cyperus alternifolius 102, 113
Cyrtomium falcatum 114

D

Daffodils 62, 110
Daffodils, potting 62
Dagger Plant 102
Damping off 89
Darlingtonia californica 106, 113
Devil's Ivy 99, 101
Devil's Tongue 110
Dieffenbachia maculata 112
Dieffenbachia picta 112
Dionaea muscipula 106, 113
Dipladenia sanderi 'Rosea' 97, 113
Diseases 88, 89
    black leg 89
    botrytis 88
    damping off 89
    physiological 90, 91
    powdery mildew 89

rusts 88
  sooty mould 88
  viruses 88
Dizygotheca elegantissima 102, 113
Donkey's Tail 101
Dracaena deremensis 103, 113
Dracaena fragrans 115
Dracaena marginata 115
Draceana terminalis 111
Dragon Tree 103
Drosera binata 107, 113
Drosera capensis 107, 113
Drosera dichotoma 107
Drosera intermedia 107
Dumb Cane 112
Dutch Hyacinth 104, 110
Dwarf Lemon 109

E
Earwigs 87
Easter Cactus 94
Elephant's Ear Philodendron 99
Elephant's Ears 113
Emerald Feather 100
Emerald Fern 100
English Ivy 98
Epipremnum aureum 99, 101
Epipremnum pinnatum 'Aureum' 99, 101, 113
Episcia cupreata 95
Episcia dianthiflora 95, 113
Euphorbia pulcherrima 111
Exacum affine 104, 111

F
Fairy Primrose 104
Falling Stars 94
False Aralia 102
False Castor Oil Plant 102
False Hop 111
Fat-headed Lizzie 98, 102
Fatshedera lizei 98, 102, 111
Fatsia japonica 102, 111
Feeding 26, 27
  air plants 27
  bromeliads 27
  foliar 26
  liquid 26
  pills 26
  sticks 26
Finger Aralia 102
Ficus benjamina 102, 113
Ficus deltoidea 102, 108, 113
Ficus diversifolia 102, 108
Ficus elastica 102, 113
Ficus lyrata 102, 113

Ficus pumila 100, 115
Fiddle-leaf Fig 102
Fishtail Fern 115
Fittonia argyroneura 101
Fittonia argyroneura nana 101
Fittonia verschaffeltii 101, 113
Fittonia verschaffeltii 'Argyroneura' 101, 113
Fittonia verschaffeltii 'Argyroneura Nana' 101, 113
Flame Lily 97
Flame Nettle 110
Flame Violet 95
Flaming Dragon Tree 111
Flaming Katy 111
Flamingo Flower 113
Flamingo Lily 112
Flamingo Plant 111
Floradora 97, 105
Florist's Cyclamen 104
Flowering climbers 96
Flowering trailers and cascading plants 94, 95
Formosa Rice Tree 102
Forster Sentry Palm 103
Fox Tail 112
Foxtail Fern 100
Freckle Face 111
Freesia 104
Freesia x hybrida 104, 111
Freesia x kewensis 104
Fruit Salad Plant 99, 103

G
Gardenia 105
Gardenia jasminoides 105, 113
German Ivy 99
German Violet 104
Giant Fork-leaved Sundew 107
Glechoma hederacea 'Variegata' 100, 113
Gloriosa rothschildiana 97, 113
Gloriosa Lily 97
Gloriosa superba 97, 113
Glory Lily, 97
Glory Flower 96
Glossy-leaved Paper Plant 102
Gold Dust Plant 110
Gold Dust Tree 110
Golden Pothos 99, 101
Golden Trumpet 96
Goldfish Plant 94
Gomozia granadensis 108
Goodluck Plant 110
Good Luck Plant 111
Goosefoot Vine 113

Grape Ivy 98
Green Pepper 108
Greenfly 84
Grevillea robusta 102, 111
Grey Mould 88
Grooming and care 28, 29
  cleaning leaves 29
  flowers 29
  stems 29
  shoots 29
  training 28
Gunpowder Plant 112
Gynura aurantiaca 101, 113
Gynura procumbens 101, 113
Gynura sarmentosa 101

H
Hanging-baskets, indoor 70, 71
  suitable plants 70
Hanging Geranium 94
Hawaiian Good Luck Plant 111
Heartleaf Philodendron 98, 101
Hearts Entangled 101
Hearts-on-a-string 101
Hedera canariensis 'Gloire de Marengo' 98
Hedera canariensis 'Variegata' 98, 113
Hedera helix 98, 113
Helxine soleirolii 101
Hen-and-chicken Fern 114
Heptapleurum arboricola 103
Herb-scented Geranium 104
Herbs, indoor 80, 81
  looking after 80, 81
  propagating 80, 81
  suitable plants 80
    chervil 80
    chives 80
    parsley 80
    pot marjoram 80
    summer savory 80
    sweet basil 80
    thyme 80
Heterocentron elegans 94
Hibiscus rosa-sinensis 111
Hippeastrum hybrida 110
Hippeastrums, potting 65
Holiday care of houseplants 82, 83
Holly Fern 115
Honey Plant 97, 105
Hooded Pitcher Plant 106
Horse's Tail 101
Hot Water Plant 96
House-blooming Mock Orange 105
House Lime 112
House Pine 102

Howeia belmoreana 103
Howeia forsteriana 103
Howea belmoreana 103, 115
Howea forsteriana 103, 115
Hoya bella 95, 105, 113
Hoya carnosa 97, 105, 113
Humidity 22, 23
  double-potting 23
  excessive 22
  mist-spraying 23
Huntsman's cup 107
Huntsman's Horn 107
Hurrican Plant 99, 103
Hyacinth 104, 110
Hyacinths 60-61
  in bulb-glasses 61
  in glass bowls 61
Hyacinthus orientalis 104, 110, 113
Hydroculture 72, 73
  suitable plants 72
Hypoestes phyllostachya 111
Hypoestes sanguinolenta 111

I
Impatiens holstii 110
Impatiens walleriana 110
India Rubber Tree 102
Indian Azalea 111
Indian Cup 107
Indoor hanging-baskets 70, 71
  planting 70, 71
  suitable plants 70
Insectiverous plants 106
Iresine herbstii 110
Irish Moss 101
Iron Cross Begonia 111
Italian Bellflower 94
Ivy Geranium 94
Ivy-tree 98, 102
Ivy-leaved Geranium 94

J
Jacob's Coat 111
Japanese Aralia 102
Japanese Fatsia 102
Japanese Holly Fern 115
Japanese Jasmine 97
Japanese Pittosporum 105
Japanese Sedum 101
Jasminum mesnyi 97, 111
Jasminum polyanthum 97, 104, 111
Jasminum primulinum 97
Java Fig 102
Justicia brandegeana 111

K
Kalanchoe blossfeldiana 112
Kangaroo Vine 98
Kentia belmoreana 103
Kentia forsteriana 103
Kentia Palm 103
King and Queen Fern 114
King Begonia 111

L
Lace Flower 95
Lace Flower Vine 95
Ladder Fern 100
Lamb's Tail 101
Lemon Geranium 104
Lemon-scented Geranium 104
Leopard Lily 112
Light 16, 17
    artificial 16
Linkleaf 94
Lipstick Vine 94
Lobster Plant 111
Lollipop Plant 113

M
Madagascar Dragon Tree 115
Madagascar Jasmine 97, 105
Madeira Ivy 98
Magic Carpet 101
Mandevilla sanderi 'Rosea' 97
Maranta leuconeura 112
Maranta makoyana 113
Mealy bugs 86
    root 86
Measles Plant 111
Mermaid Vine 98
Mexican Flameleaf 111
Mexican Shrimp Plant 111
Meyer Lemon 109
Mikania ternata 100, 113
Mind Your Own Business 101
Miniature Wax Flower 95, 105
Mint Geranium 104
Miracle Plant 98, 102
Mistletoe Fig 102, 108
Mistletoe Rubber Fig 102, 108
Mites 86
    cyclamen 86
    red spider 86
Mock Orange 105
Moisture-indicator strips 18
Moisture-meters 19
Monkey-faced Pansy 96
Monstera deliciosa 99, 103, 113
Mosaic Plant 101

Mother Fern 114
Mother-in-Law Plant 113
Mother-in-Law's Tongue 110
Mother of Thousands 101
Mother Spleenwort 114
Mother's Tears 96

N
Natal Ivy 99
Nephrolepis exaltata 100, 113
Nephrolepis exaltata 'Bostoniensis' 100, 113
Nephthytis 99
Nerium oleander 104
Nertera depressa 108, 111
Nertera granadensis 108
Nerve Plant 101
Never Never Plant 112
New Zealand Cliff Brake 100
Norfolk Island Pine 102
Nutmeg Geranium 104

O
Oilcloth Flower 112
Oleander 104
Oplismenus hirtellus 100, 111
Ornamental Pepper 99, 108

P
Pachystachys lutea 113
Painted Leaf 101
Painted Leaf Begonia 112
Painted Leaves 110
Painted Nettle 110
Painter's Palette 112
Panama Orange 108
Paper Flower 96
Paper Plant 102
Paradise Palm 103
Parasol Plant 103
Parlor Ivy 99
Passiflora caerulea 97, 111
Patient Lucy 110
Peace Lily 113
Peacock Plant 113
Pelargonium capitatum 104, 111
Pelargonium crispum 104, 111
Pelargonium x fragrans 104, 111
Pelargonium graveolens 104, 111
Pelargonium peltatum 94, 111
Pelargonium tomentosum 104, 111
Pellaea rotundifolia 100, 113
Peperomia scandens 'Variegata' 101
Peppermint Geranium 104
Persian Violet 104
Pests 84-87

aphides 84
aphids 84
aphis 84
blackfly 84
controlling 84, 85
cyclamen mites 86
earwigs 87
greenfly 84
mealy bugs 86
preventing 84
red spider mites 86
root mealy bugs 86
scale insects 86
slugs 87
snails 87
thrips 86
vine weevils 87
whitefly 86
Philippine Medusa 112
Philodendron andreanum 99
Philodendron domestica 99, 113
Philodendron erubescens 99, 113
Philodendron hastatum 99
Philodendron melanochrysum 99, 113
Philodendron pertusum 99, 103
Philodendron scandens 98, 101, 115
Phoenix canariensis 103, 113
Physiological disorders 90, 91
    flower buds falling off 90
    green shoots 90
    leaves falling off 90
    wilting 90
Pickaback Plant 110
Piggyback Plant 110
Pigtail Anthurium 113
Pigtail Plant 113
Pilea cadierei 112
Pilea microphylla 112
Pilea muscosa 112
Pink Allamanda 97
Pink Dot 111
Pink Jasmine 97, 104
Piper crocatum 99, 113
Pitcher Plant 107
Pittosporum tobira 105, 113
Plectranthus australis 101, 113
Plectranthus coleoides 'Marginatus' 101, 113
Plectranthus oertendahlii 101, 113
Plectranthus parviflorus 101
Plumbago auriculata 97, 111
Plumbago capensis 97
Plume Asparagus 100
Plush Vine 100
Pocketbook Flower 112
Poinsettia 111

Polka-dot Plant 111
Poor Man's Orchid 110
Pothos aureus 99
Pothos Vine 99, 101
Pots 14, 15
    cache 14
    clay 14
    plastic 14
    range of sizes 14
    saucers 14
Potting 32, 33
Pouch Flower 112
Powdery Mildew 89
Prayer Plant 112
Pricking off seedlings 32, 33
Primrose Jasmine 97
Primula 104
Primula x kewensis 104, 111
Primula malacoides 104, 111
Propagation 30-59
    air-layering 38, 39
        suitable plants 38
    cacti 30, 56, 57
    cane cuttings 58, 59
        horizonal 58
        vertical 59
    cross-sections of leaves 54, 55
        suitable plants 54
    cuttings 42-59
    division 34, 35
        suitable plants 34
    heel-cuttings 43
    layering 36, 37
        suitable plants 36
    leaf-petiole cuttings 46, 47
    leaf-squares 52, 53
        suitable plants 52
    leaf-triangles 50, 51
        suitable plants 50
    plantlets 40, 41
        suitable plants 40
    rooting cuttings in water 46
    runners 40, 41
        suitable plants 40
    seeds 30, 31
        helping to germinate 30
        sowing 31
        suitable plants 30
            cacti 30
            ferns 30
            flowering 30
            foliage 30
            fruiting 30
            insectiverous 30
            palms 30

succulents 30
stem cuttings 44, 45
stem-tip cuttings 42, 43
succulents 56, 57
ti-cuttings 58, 59
whole-leaf cuttings 48, 49
suitable plants 48
Prostrate Coleus 101
Purple Heart 101
Purple Passion Flower 101

R

Rat's Tail Cactus 94
Rattail Cactus 94
Red-leaf Philodendron 99
Red Pepper 108
Red spider mites 86
Repotting 24, 25
Rex Begonia 112
Rhaphidophora aurea 99
Rhipsalidopsis gaertneri 94, 111
Rhipsalis baccifera 108
Rhipsalis cassutha 108, 111
Rhododendron simsii 111
Rhoeo discolor 112
Rhoeo spathacea 112
Rhoicissus rhomboidea 98
Rhoicissus rhomboidea 'Ellen Danica' 98
Ribbon Plant 100
Root mealy bugs 86
Rosary Vine 101
Rosebay 104
Rose Geranium 104
Rose of China 111
Rose-scented Geranium 104
Rubber Plant 102

S

Saffron Plant 112
Saintpaulia grotei 94, 113
Sansevieria trifasciata 110
Sarracenia x catesbaei 107
Sarracenia flava 107, 113
Sarracenia hybrida 107
Sarracenia purpurea 107, 113
Saxifraga sarmentosa 'Tricolor' 101
Saxifraga stolonifera 'Tricolor' 101, 113
Scale insects 86
Scarborough Lily 111
Scented houseplants 104
Schefflera actinophylla 102
Schefflera arboricola 103, 113
Schizanthus pinnatus 110
Schizocentron elegans 94, 113
Schlumbergera 'Buckleyi' 94, 111

Schlumbergera gaertneri 94
Schlumbergera hybrida 94
Schlumbergera truncata 94, 111
Scindapsus aureus 99, 101
Sedum morganianum 101, 111
Sedum sieboldii mediovariegatum 101, 111
Selecting and buying houseplants 12, 13
acclimatizing new houseplants 13
Senecio cruentus 112
Senecio macroglossus 'Variegatus' 99, 113
Senecio mikanioides 99
Senecio rowleyanus 101, 105, 111
Sentry Palm 103
Setcreasea pallida 'Purple Heart' 101, 111
Shrimp Begonia 94
Shrimp Plant 111
Side-saddle Flower 107
Silk Oak 102
Silky Oak 102
Silver Nerve 101
Silver Net Leaf 101
Silver Net Plant 101
Silvery Inch Plant 101
Slipper Flower 112
Slipperwort 112
Slugs 87
Snake Plant 110
Small-leaved Rubber Plant 102
Snails 87
Snakeskin Plant 101
Solanum capsicastrum 108, 111
Sooty mould 88
Spade-leaf Philodendron 99
Spanish Bayonet 102
Spanish Shawl 94
Sparmannia africana 112
Spathe Flower 113
Spathiphyllum wallisii 113
Spice Berry 102, 104, 108
Spider Ivy 100
Spider Plant 100
Spineless Yucca 102
Spiraea 110
Split-leaf Philodendron 99, 103
Soleirolia soleirolii 101, 113
Spotted Dumb Cane 112
Spotted Laurel 110
Star of Bethlehem 94
Stephanotis floribunda 97, 105, 113
Strap Flower 113
Strawberry Begonia 101
Strawberry Geranium 101
String of Hearts 101
String of Beads 101, 105
Striped Inch Plant 100

Succulents 110
Sultana 110
Sundew 107
Swedish Begonia 101
Swedish Ivy 101
Sweetheart Plant 98, 101
Sweet-scented Geranium 104
Swiss Cheese Plant 99, 103
Sword Fern 100
Syngonium podophyllum 99, 115

T

Taro Vine 99, 101
Ten Commandments 112
Terraria 68, 69
planting 68, 69
suitable plants 68
Thanksgiving Cactus 94
Thatch-leaf Palm 103
Thousand Mothers 110
Thrips 86
Thunbergia alata 96, 111
Ti Plant 111
Tolmiea menziesii 110
Top-dressing 27
Tradescantia fluminensis 101, 111
Trailing African Violet 94
Tree of Kings 111
Trichosporum lobbianum 94
Trichosporum speciosum 94
Trumpet Leaf 107
Tulips, 63, 110
potting 63

U

Umbrella Grass 102
Umbrella Palm 102
Umbrella Plant 102
Umbrella Sedge 102
Umbrella Tree 102
Umbrella Trumpets 107

V

Vacation care 82, 83
Vallota purpurea 111
Vallota speciosa 111
Variegated Candle Flower 101
Variegated Ground Ivy 100
Variegated Laurel 111
Velvet Plant 101
Venezuela Treebine 98
Venus Fly Trap 106
Vine weevils 87
Viruses 88

W

Walking Anthericum 100
Wandering Jew 101
Warmth 16
Watches 107
Water Ivy 99
Watering 18, 19
applying water 19
judging if water is needed 18, 19
need for water 18–21
saving a dry plant 20, 21
saving an excessively watered plant 20, 21
Watermelon Pilea 112
Wax Flower 97, 105
Wax Ivy 99
Wax Plant 97, 105
Weeping Fig 102
Whitefly 86
Widow's Tears 96
Wilting 20, 21
too little water 20
too much water 20
Winter Cherry 108
Woolflower 110

Y

Yellow Jasmine 97
Yellow Pitcher Plant 107
Yoke Cactus 94
Youth-on-age 110
Yucca aloifolia 102, 111
Yucca elephantipes 102, 111

Z

Zanzibar Balsam 110
Zebra Plant 112
Zebrina pendula 101, 111
Zygocactus truncatus 94

ACKNOWLEDGEMENTS

The publishers gratefully acknowledge the invaluable assistance provided by the following,
without whom this book would not have been possible:

Barnsfold Nurseries, Tismans Common, Sussex
Chessington Nurseries – Des Whitwell, Daphne, Ian and Wayne
Clarke and Spiers, Ripley, Surrey – Keith Francis, Rosalind Reeves, Felicity Wilcox and Douglas Hammond
Forest Lodge Garden Centre, Farnham, Surrey – Steven Oaten
Hollygate Cactus Nursery, Ashington, Sussex – Terry Hewitt
Secrett Garden Centre, Milford, Surrey – Robert and Gill Secrett and Jane Barney
Allan Smith Nurseries, Titchfield, Hants – Allan and June Smith
Vesutor Air Plants, Billingshurst, Sussex
Hand modelling by Angela Taylor, Diana Letts and Fiona Sutherland

Editor David Gibbon
Typesetting Julie Smith
Design Claire Leighton
Director of Production Gerald Hughes